START
BIG
ENGLISH

Linnette Ansel • Lisa Broomhead

Mario Herrera • Christopher Sol Cruz

PUPIL'S BOOK

Contents

Structures	I can ...
Hello. / Goodbye. What's your name? My name's (Lidya). How old are you? I'm (six). What's your favourite colour? My favourite colour is (red). What's this? It's a book. It's a (black) book.	
Who's this? This is my (mum). / This is me.	... talk about family. ... help my family.
It's my birthday! Happy birthday! Is it a (car)? Yes, it is. / No, it isn't. It's a (car).	... ask and answer about toys. ... talk about birthday parties and locations around town. ... speak politely.
I like (pizza). / I don't like (water). Pizza, please.	... talk about foods I like and don't like. ... talk about healthy and unhealthy foods. ... identify good table manners.
I've got (two eyes) and (a nose). Have you got (long hair/blue eyes)? Yes, I have. / No, I haven't.	... talk about my body. ... describe how to wash my hands. ... brush my teeth and hair.
What are you doing? I'm (running) to the (school). Is this the (playground)? Yes, it is. / No, it isn't. It's the (hospital).	... ask and answer about actions. ... talk about vehicles and places around town. ... help keep the environment clean.
What's he/she doing? He's/She's (swinging) on the (swings). Be careful!	... ask and answer about playing at the playground. ... describe a tree in different seasons. ... help keep the park clean.
It's (sunny). What are you wearing? I'm wearing a (hat). What's he/she wearing? He's/She's wearing (trousers).	... ask and answer about clothes. ... describe the weather. ... talk about jobs and uniforms.
Where are you? I'm in the (living room). Where is he/she? She's/He's in the (hall). Ask Mum.	... talk about different rooms and ask where people are. ... describe the material things are made of. ... stay safe at home.
A (crocodile) can (swim). I can't (fly).	... talk about animals and their abilities. ... say where animals live. ... say zoo rules.

Welcome to class!

1:02 1 Listen and find.

1:03 2 Listen and find. Sing.

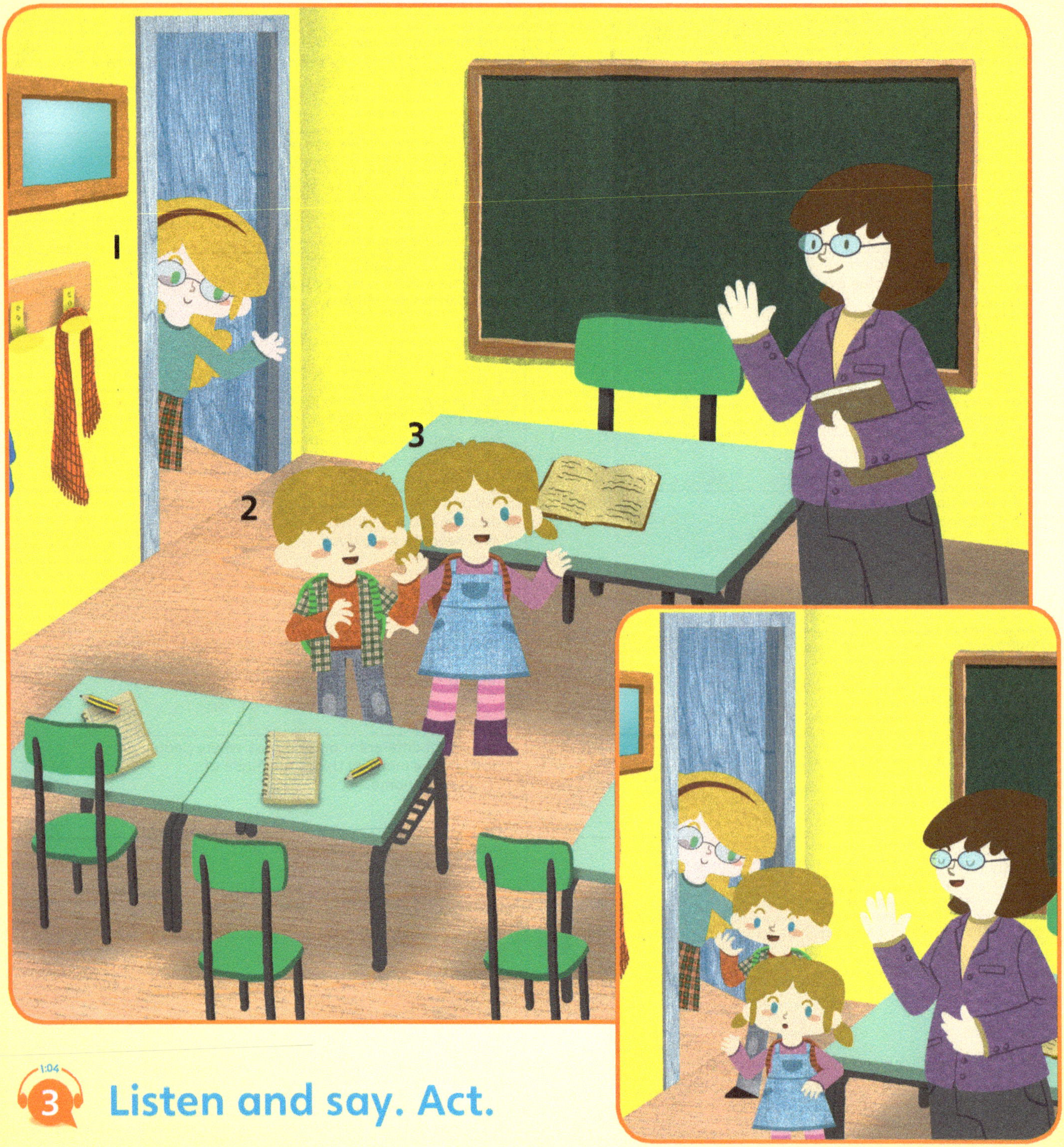

1:04 3 Listen and say. Act.

| 1 | 2 | 3 | 4 | 5 |
| 6 | 7 | 8 | 9 | 10 |

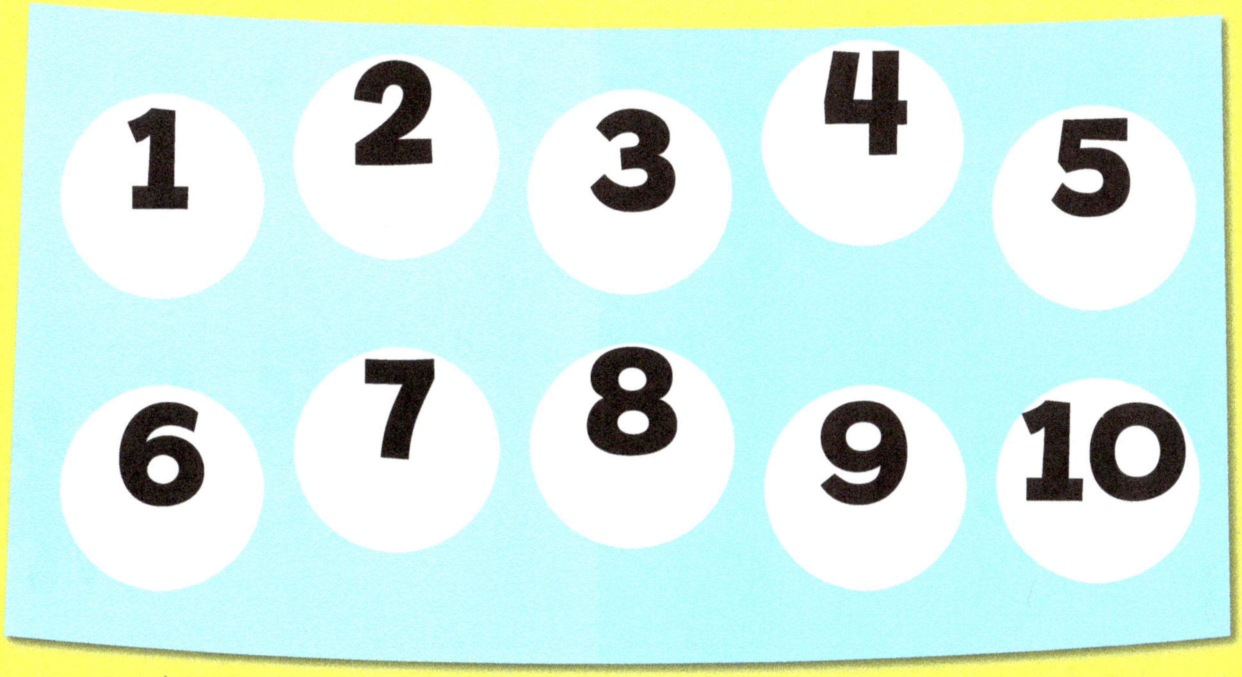

6 🎧 **Listen and find. Ask and answer.**

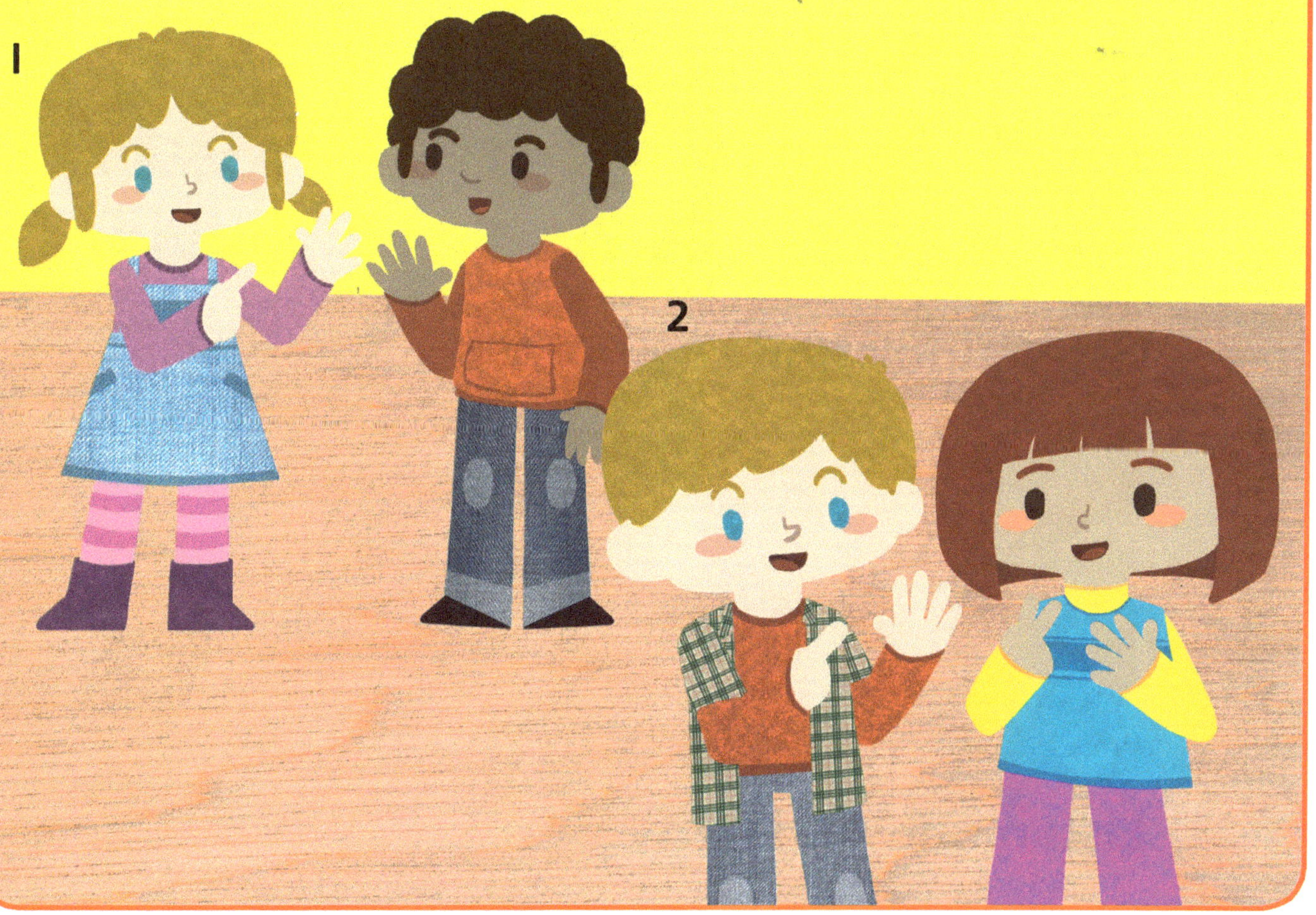

1

2

Colours

1   2   3   4

6   7   8   9

5

 **9** Listen, look and say. Ask and answer.

1   2   3

 **10** Listen, look and say.

1   2   3

4   5   6

 **11** Listen and find. Play.

 **Listen, look and say. Do.**

1
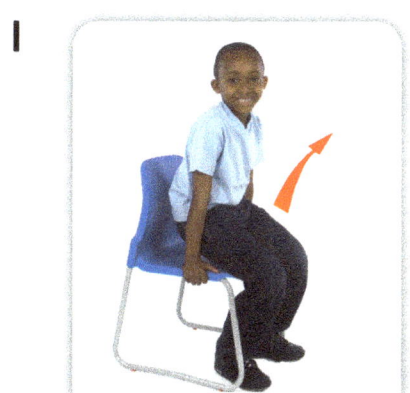

2
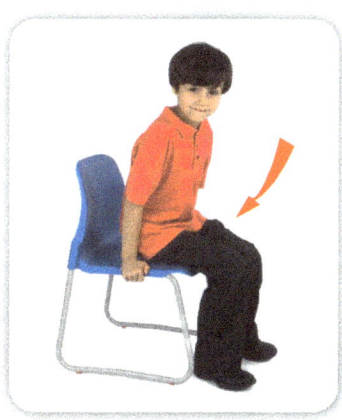

3

4

5

6

 Play.

unit 1 My Family

1:17
1 Listen, look and say.

1

2 3

4 5

6 7

8

1:18
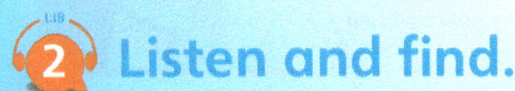
2 Listen and find.

3 Play a game.

4 Listen and find. Sing. ♪

5 Listen and say yes or no.

1  2  3  4

THINK BIG   Who's this? Say.

6 Listen and follow. Who's *Liam*?

7 Look, listen and number.

a

b

c

1

d

Language in Action

1:25
8 Listen. Help Sam and Liam.

1:26
9 Listen and ✓ or ✗.

1

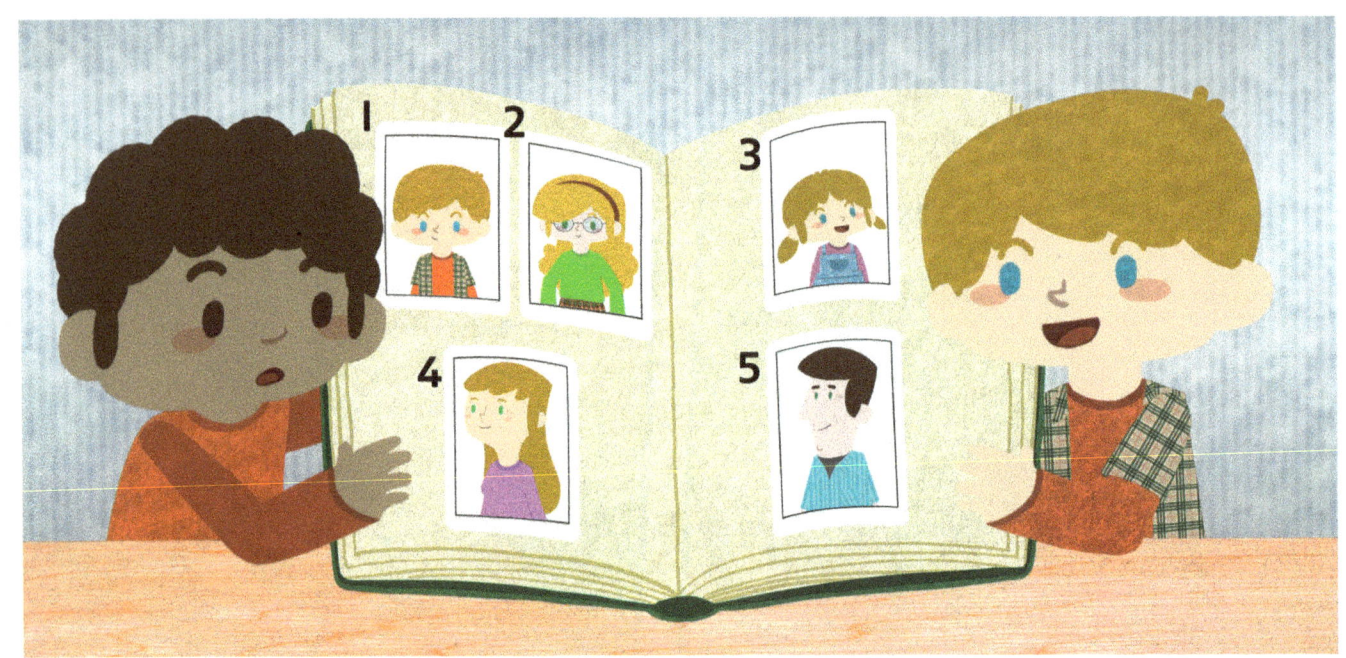

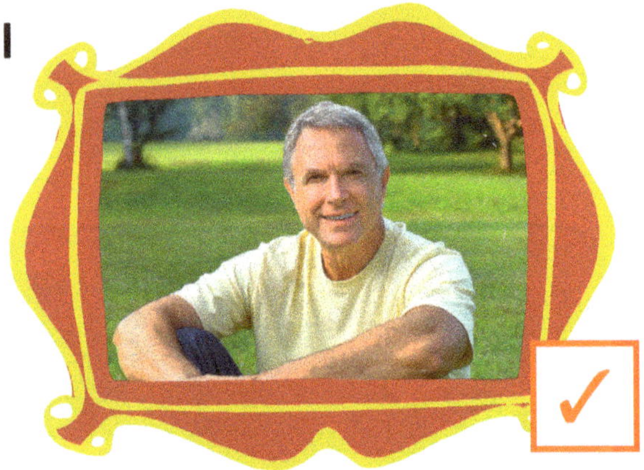

2

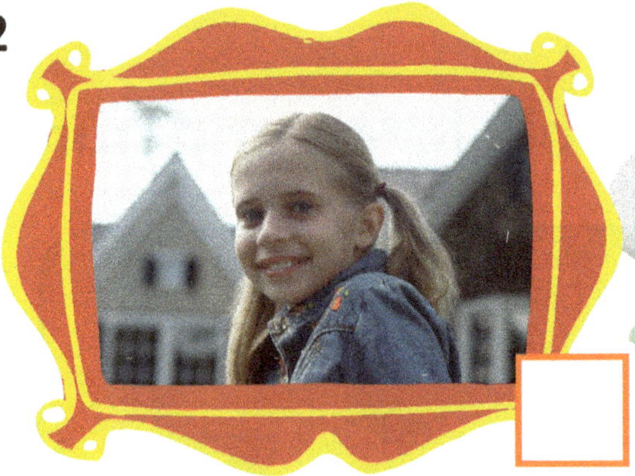

3

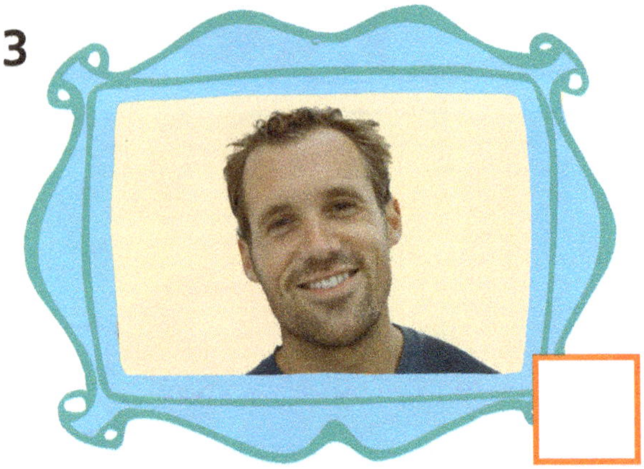

4

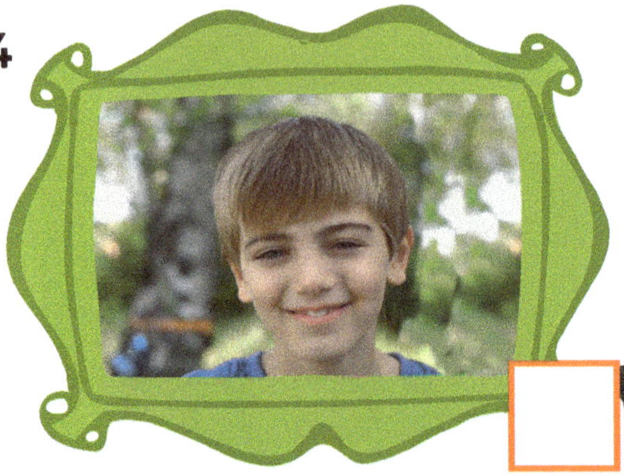

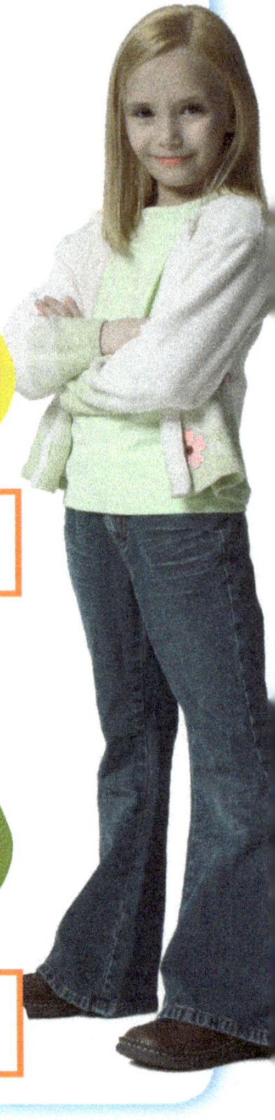

10 **Listen and number.**

11 **Draw and play.**

Review

12 Listen and follow.

1:37

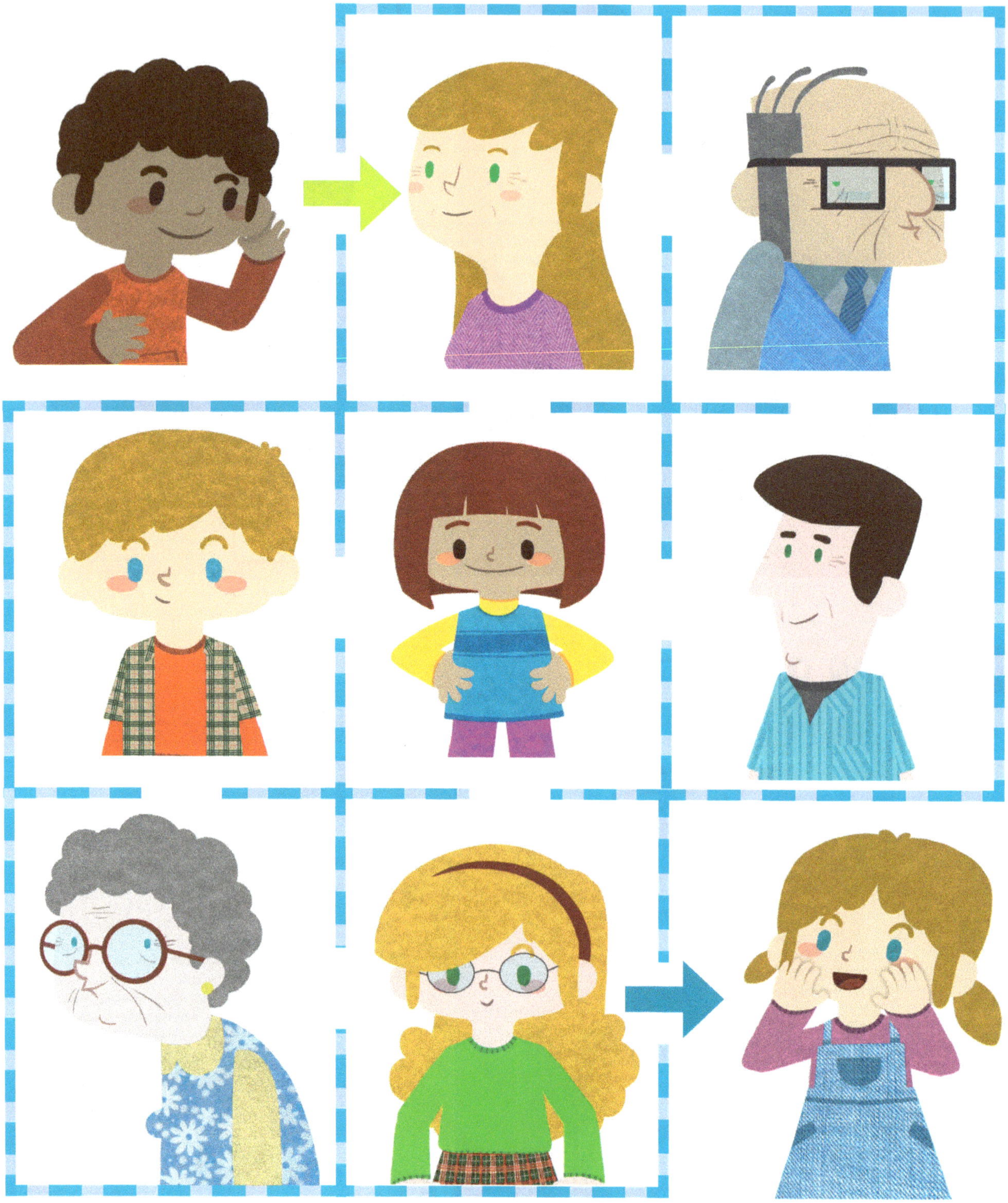

13 Play.

14 Listen and ✓ or ✗.

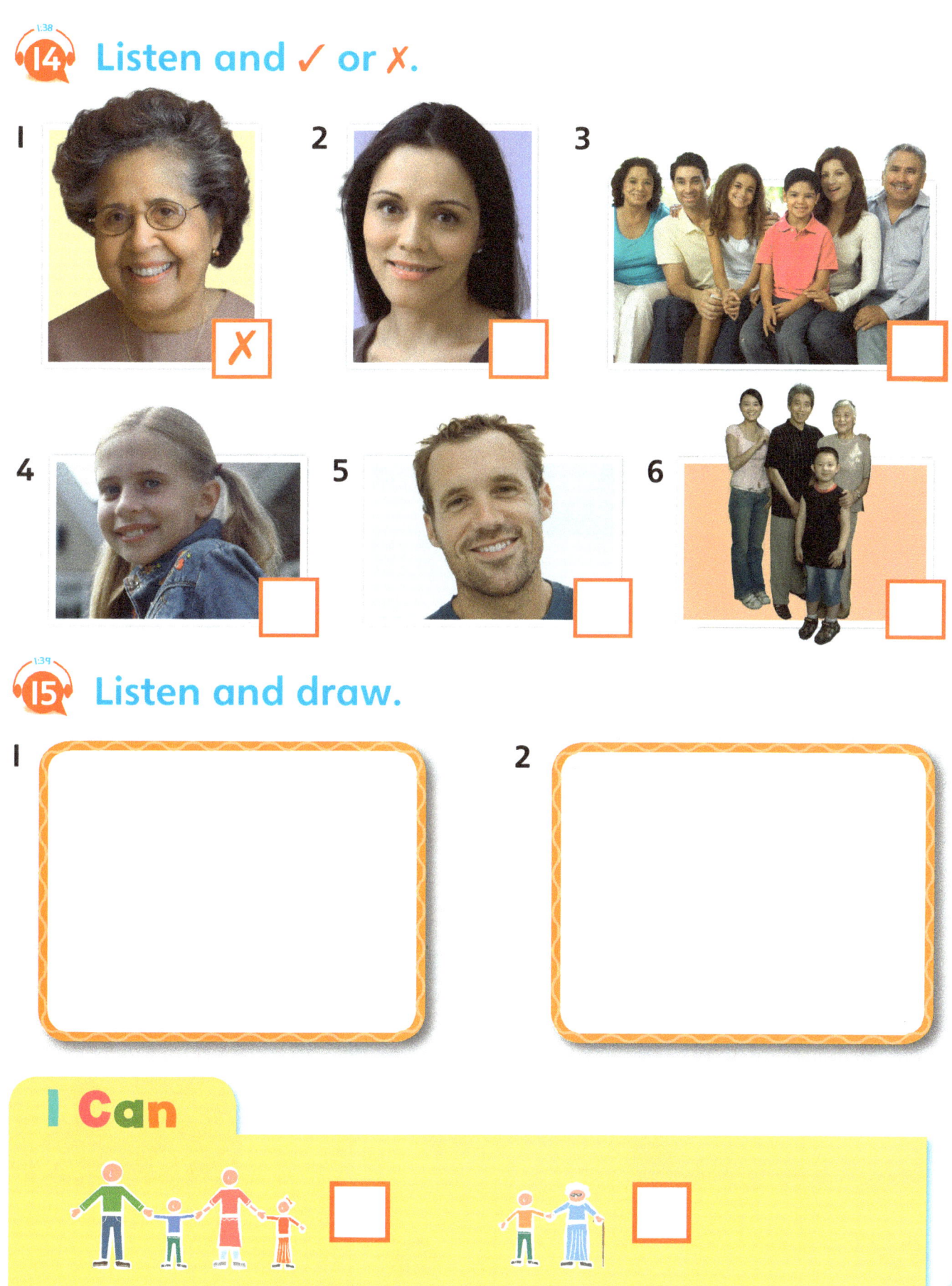

1 ✗

2

3

4

5

6

15 Listen and draw.

1

2

I Can

unit 2 Happy Birthday!

1 Listen, look and say.

2 Listen and find.   **3** Play a game.

4 Listen and ✓. Sing.

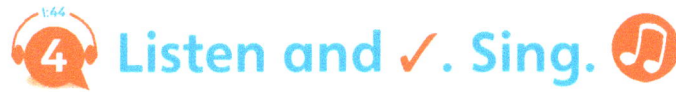

1

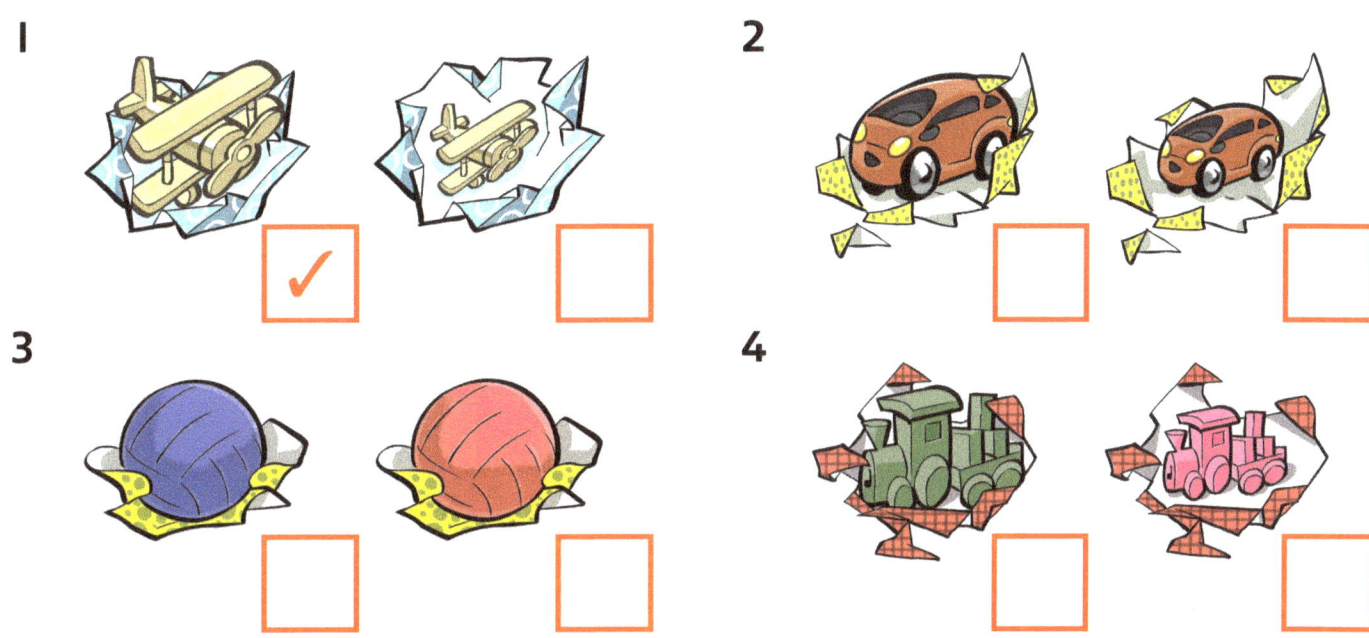

2

3

4

5 Find the differences.

1

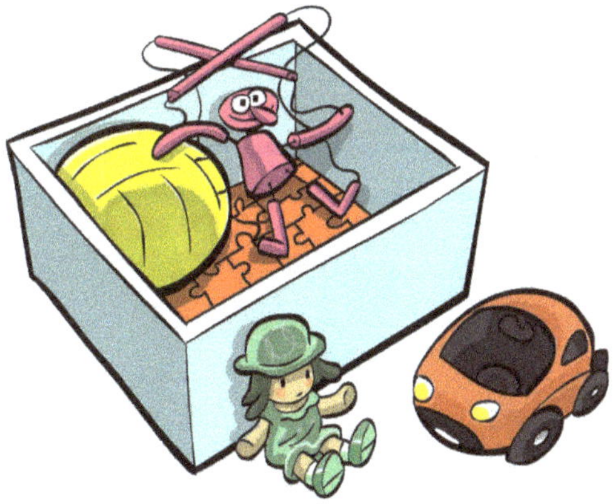

2

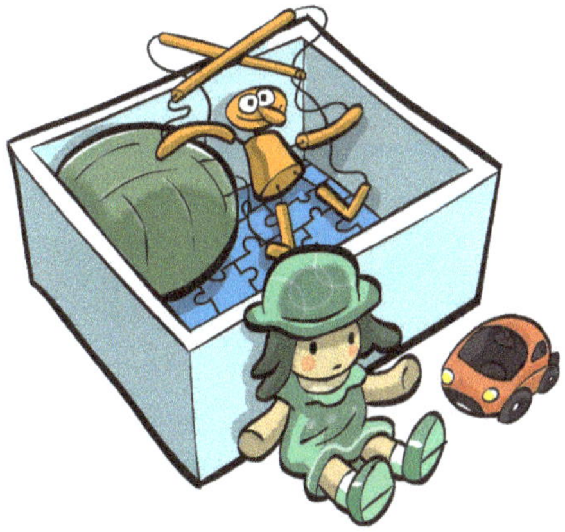

THINK BIG Say the favourite toys.

1

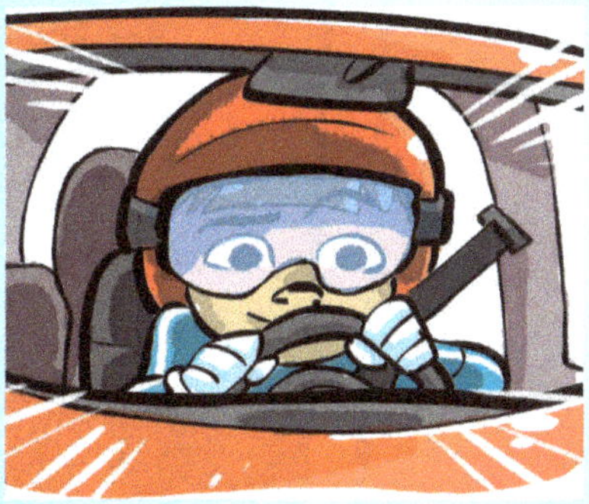

2

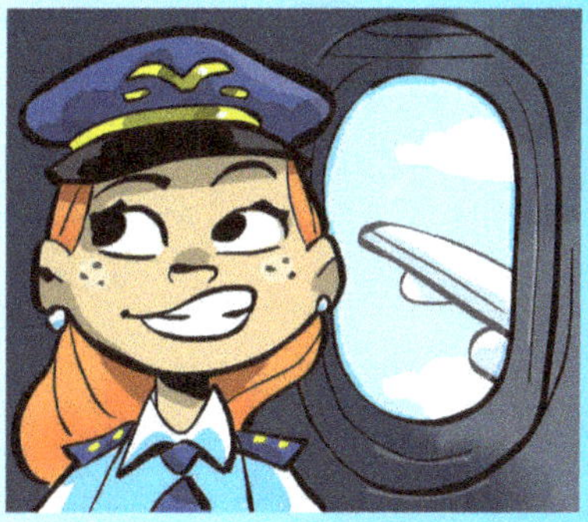

Story

6 🎧 1:46 **Listen and follow. What is each present?**

18   Unit 2

7 **Look and match. Say.**

1

2

a

b

c

d

Language in Action

8 Listen. Help Lidya and Liam.

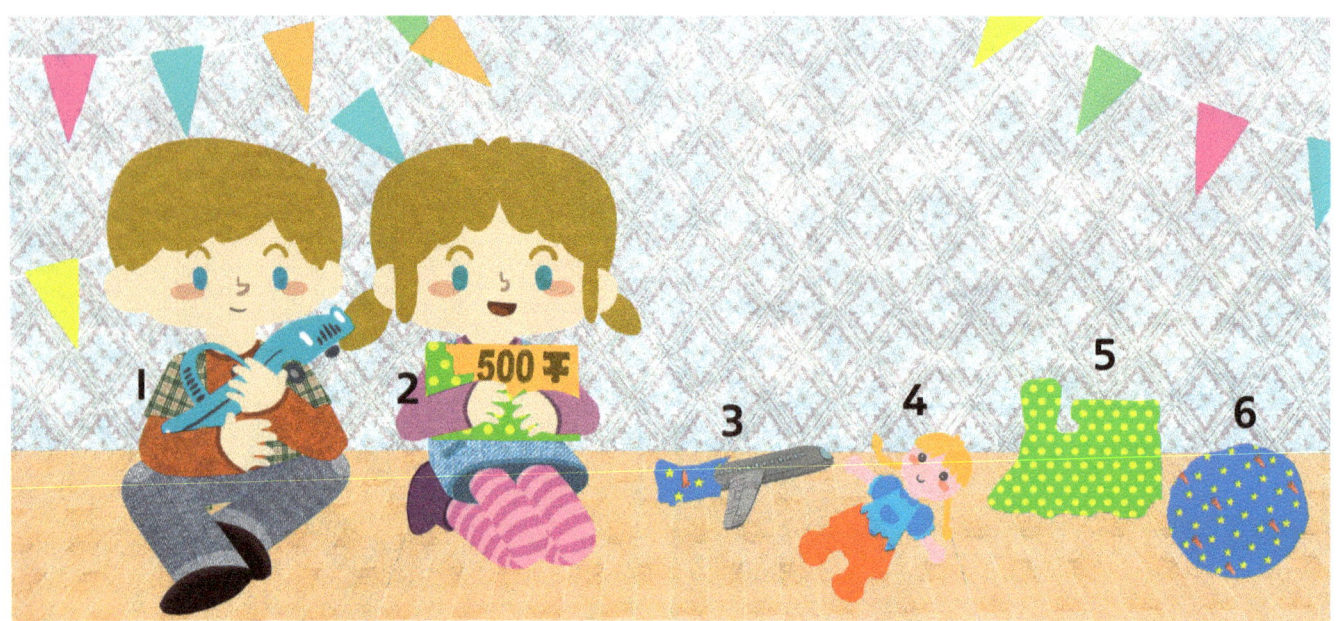

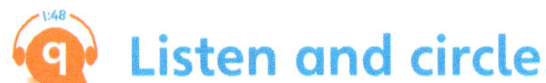

9 Listen and circle.

1 a

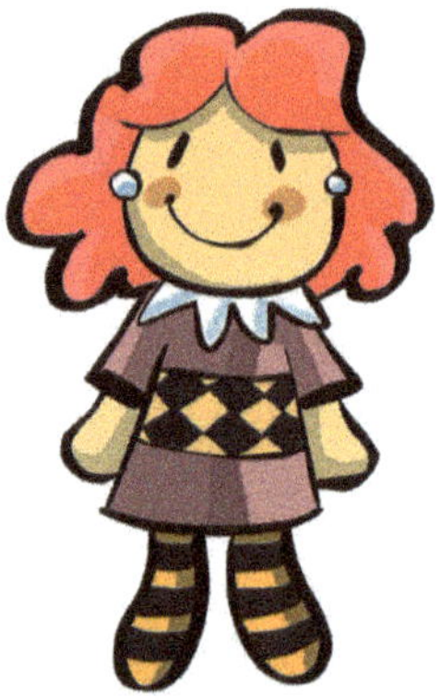

b

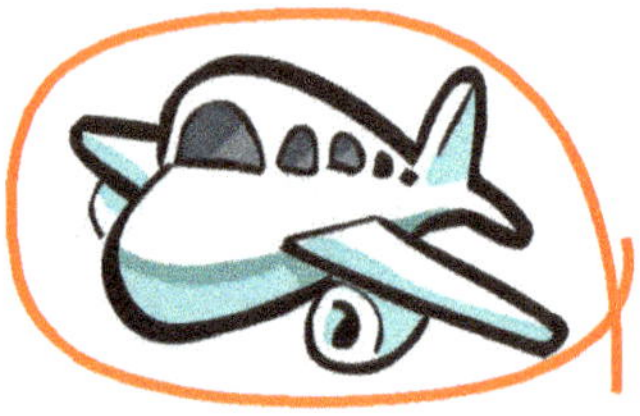

2 a

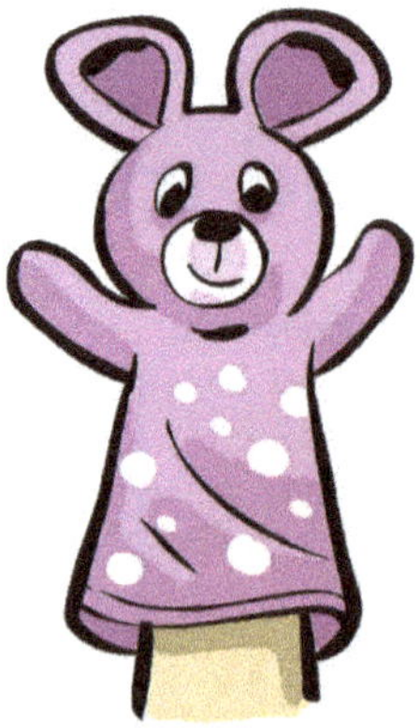

b

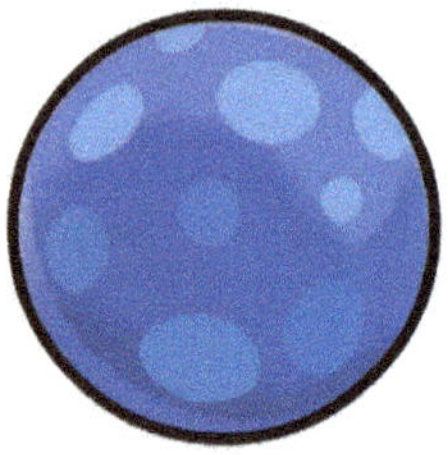

3 a

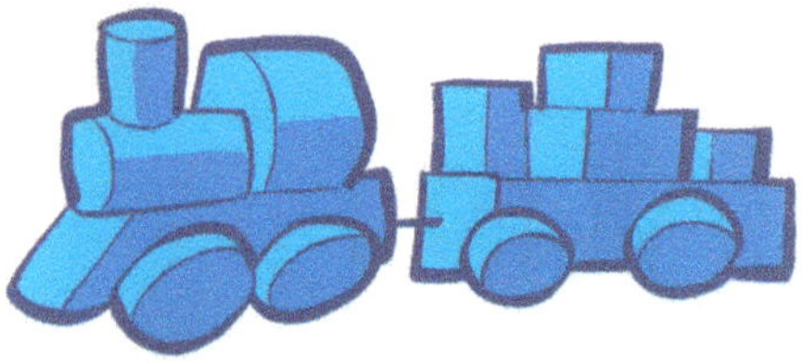

b

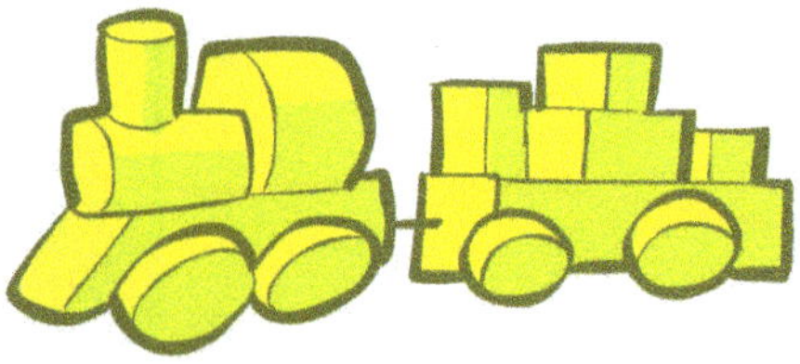

4 a

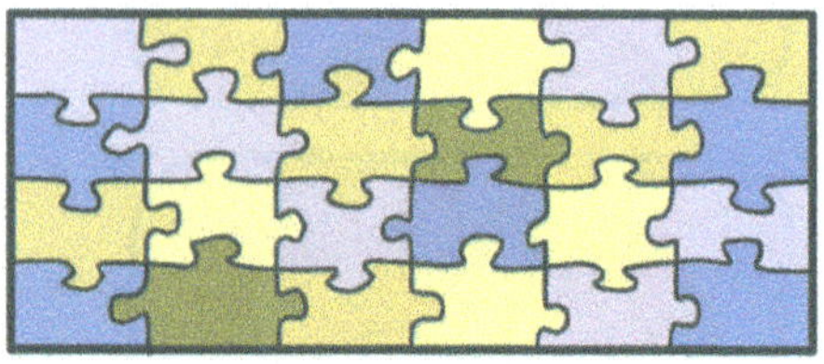

b

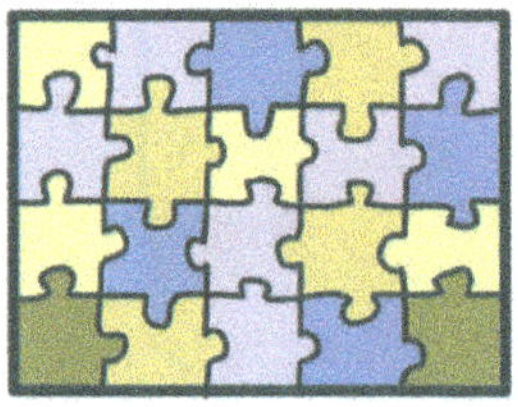

 **Listen and number. Ask and answer.**

a  ☐

b  ☐

c  ☐

d  1

 **Ask and draw.**

Me	1	2

language practice (*What's your favourite toy? My favourite toy is a plane.*)   Unit 2   21

Review

1:62

12 Listen and find.

1	2	3
	50₮ 2000₮	

4	5	6

7	8	9

13 Play. Draw o or x.

 **Listen and number.**

a

b

c  **1**

d

e

f

 Listen and draw.

1

2

I Can

unit 3 I like cake!

1 Listen, look and say.

1

2

3

4

5

6

7

8

2 Listen and find.

3 Play a game.

4 Listen and ✓. Sing. ♪

5 Listen and draw.

THINK BIG Draw the food you like.

6 Listen and follow. What does each person like?

7 Look and listen again. Circle.

7 Look and listen again. Circle.

1   a   b   c

2   a   b   c

3   a   b   c

story   Unit 3   27

Language in Action

8 Listen. Help Lidya and Liam.

9 Listen and circle.

 **10** **Listen and ✓ or ✗. Say and guess.**

1

2

3

 Play the game.

1 = 🙂   2 = 🙂

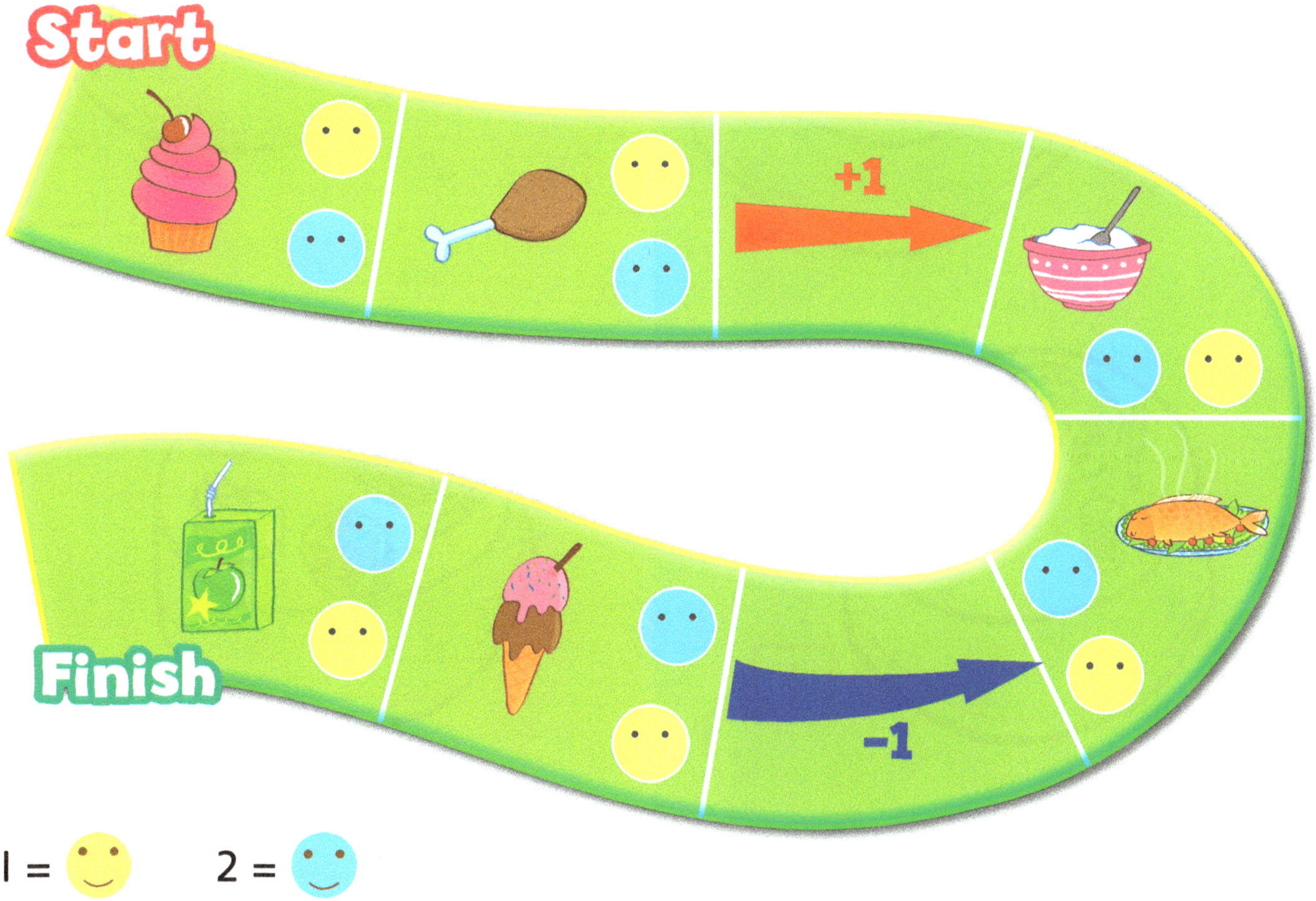

 **Listen and number.**

a

b

c
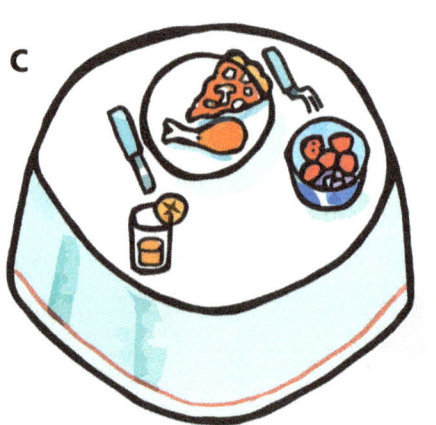

d

e

1

f

 **Play.**

14 1.86 🎧 Listen and circle.

1

2

3

4

5

6

15 Draw and say.

1   2   3   4 ❤️ ❌

I Can

My Body

1 Listen, look and say.

2 Listen and find.   **3** Play a game.

4 Listen and find. Sing. ♪

1

2

3

5 Listen and number. Say and guess.

a

b

☐

c

☐

d

☐ 1 ☐

THINK BIG Look and match.

a

b

c

6 Listen and follow. What colour is Lidya's nose?

1

2

3

4

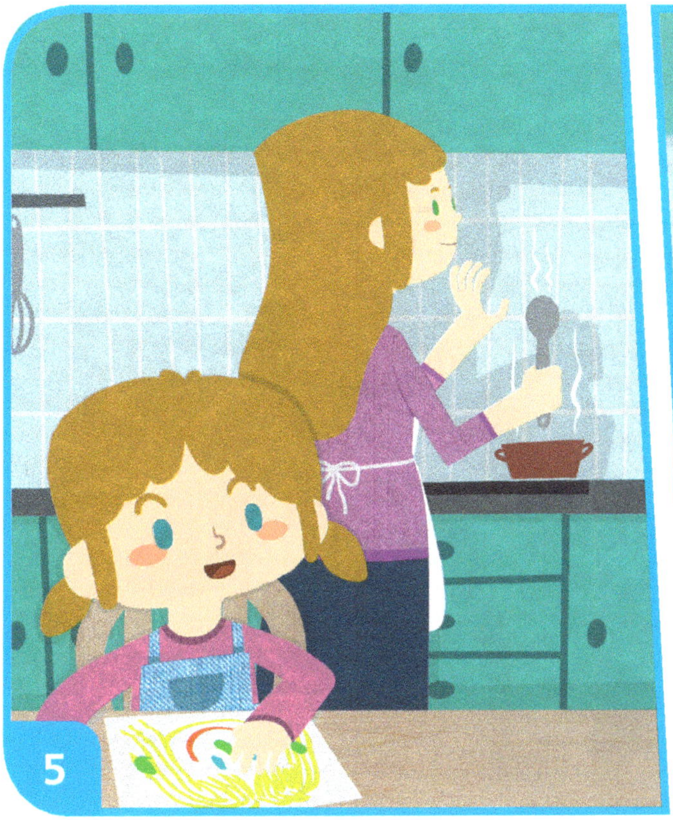

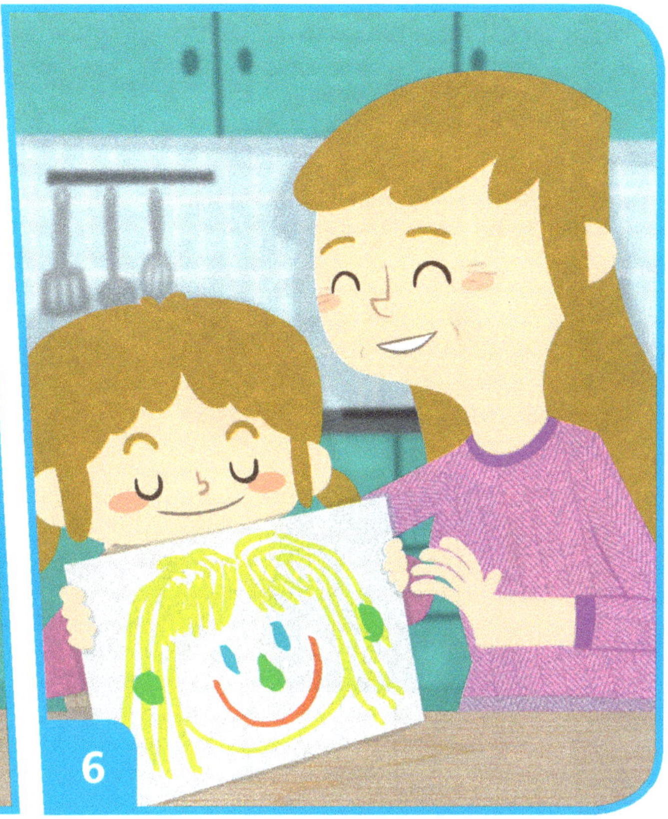

7 Listen and colour. Look and circle.

1

2

8 Listen. Help Sally and Lidya.

9 Listen and number.

a

b

c

d

1

10 Listen, circle and ✓.

11 Draw. Ask and answer.

Review

2:25 12 Listen and follow. Say the colour.

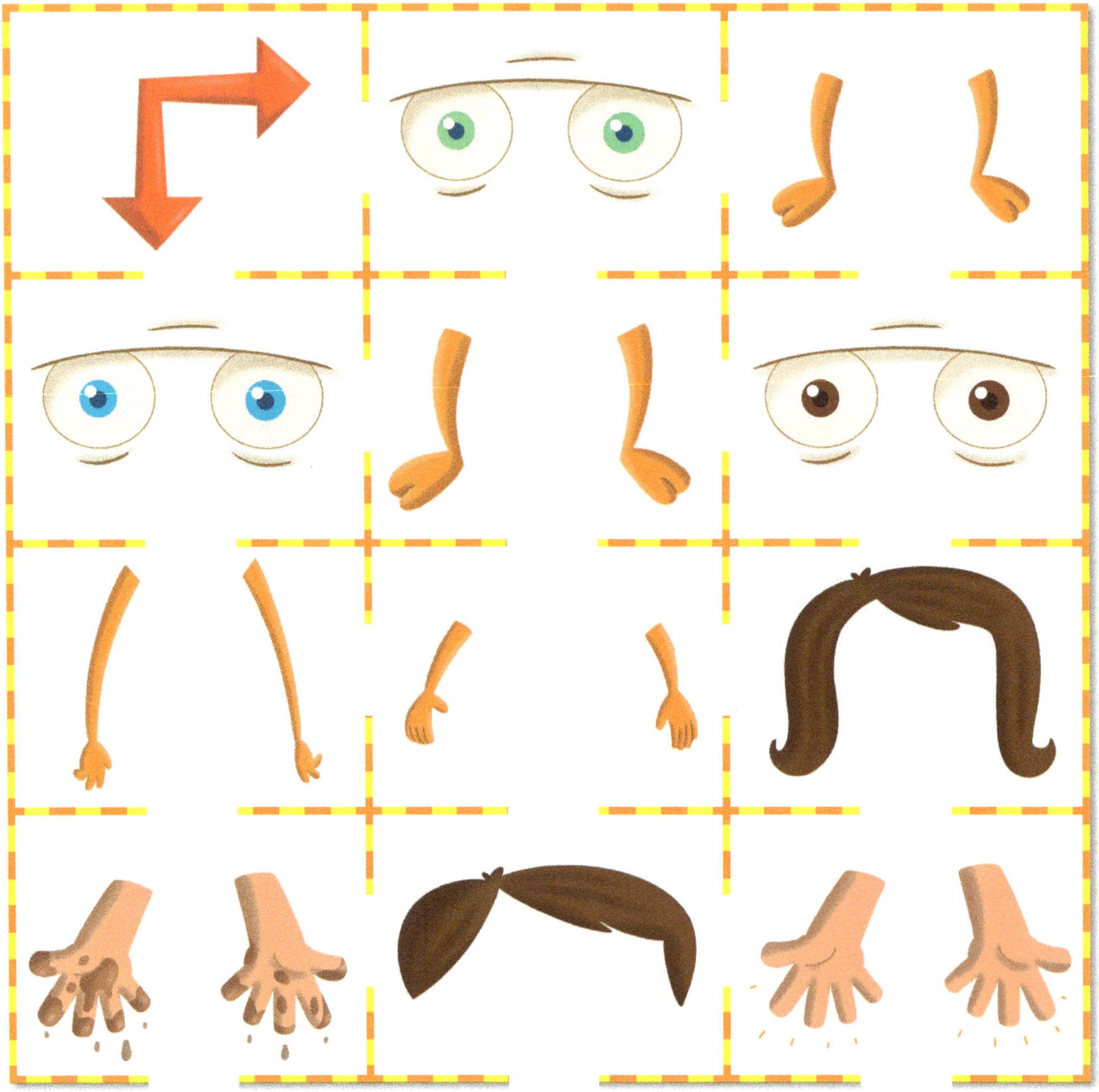

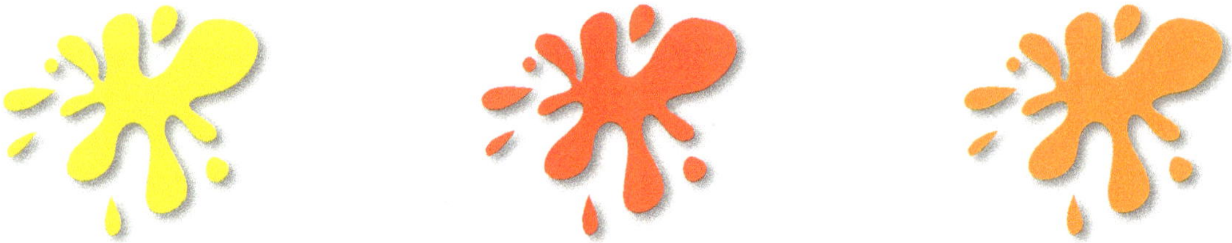

13 Play.

Listen and ✓ or ✗.

1
 ✗

2

3

4

 **Listen and number.**

a

b

c

I Can

1 Listen, look and say.

2 Listen and find.

3 Play a game.

 **4** **Listen and say the colour. Sing and do.**

5 **Listen and match. Say and guess.**

1

2

3

4

a

b

c

d

THINK BIG   **Say the places.**

1

2

Story

2:35
6 Listen and follow. What's Lidya doing?

1

2

3

4

5

6

 7 **Listen and circle.**

1 a    b

2 a    b

3 a    b

8 **Listen. Help Sam and Liam.**

 9 **Listen and match. Draw and say.**

10 Listen and draw. Play.

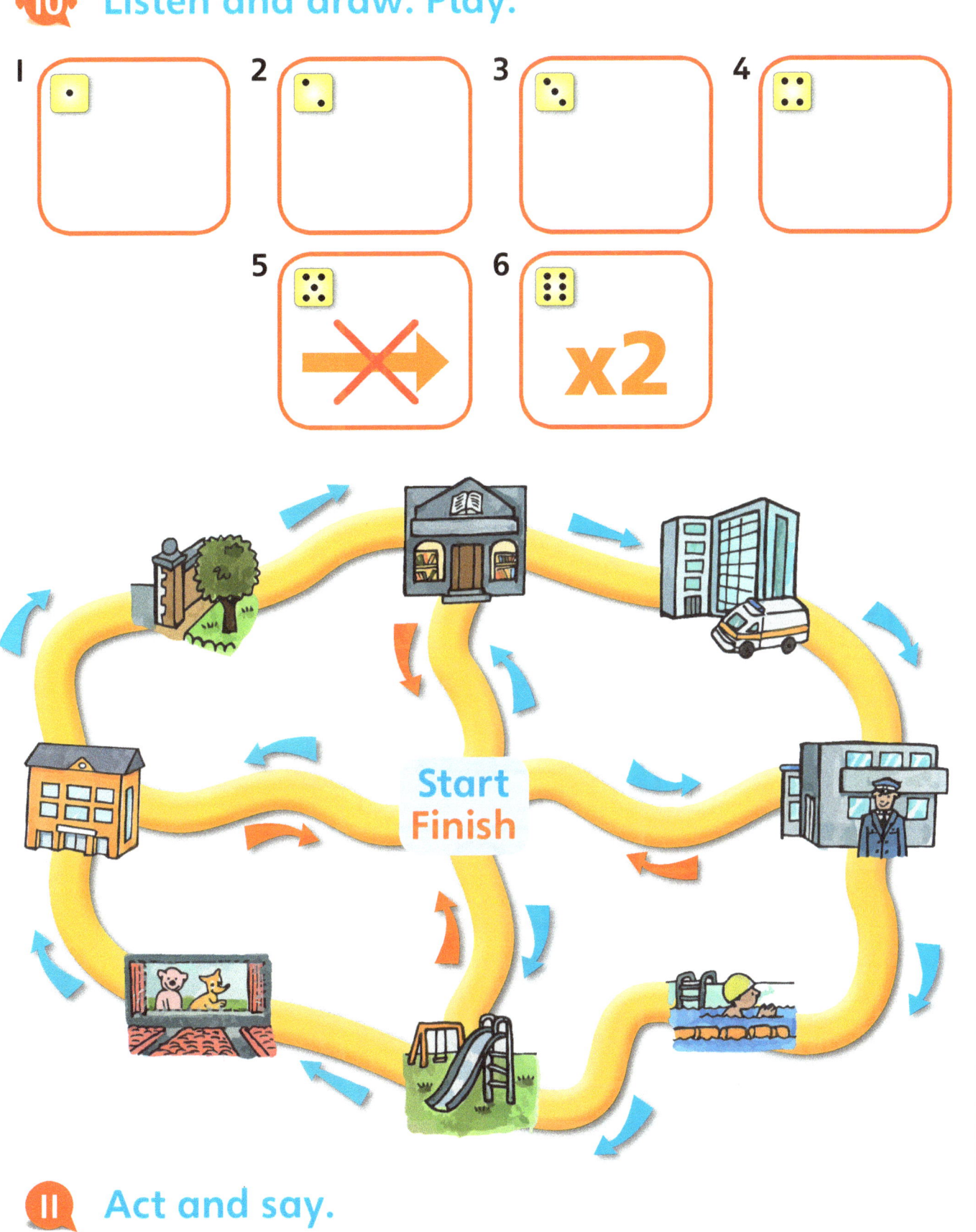

1 ·
2 ··
3 ···
4 ::
5 :·: →✗→
6 ::: x2

Start Finish

11 Act and say.

Review

12 **Listen and find.**

1

2

3

4

5

6

7

8

q

13 **Play. Draw o or x.**

Listen and ✓ or ✗.

1  ✓

2

3

4

5

6

15 Draw and say.

1

2

I Can

unit 6

She's swinging on the swings!

2 Listen and find.   **3** Play a game.

48   Unit 6   vocabulary (playground equipment)

4 Listen and number in order. Sing. 🎵

5 Look at **4** and say.

THINK BIG   Draw and say.

1

2

3

4

Story

6 Listen and follow. What's Lidya doing wrong?

7 Look and ✓ or ✗.

1 a  b

2 a b

Language in Action

8 Listen. Help Joy and Lidya.

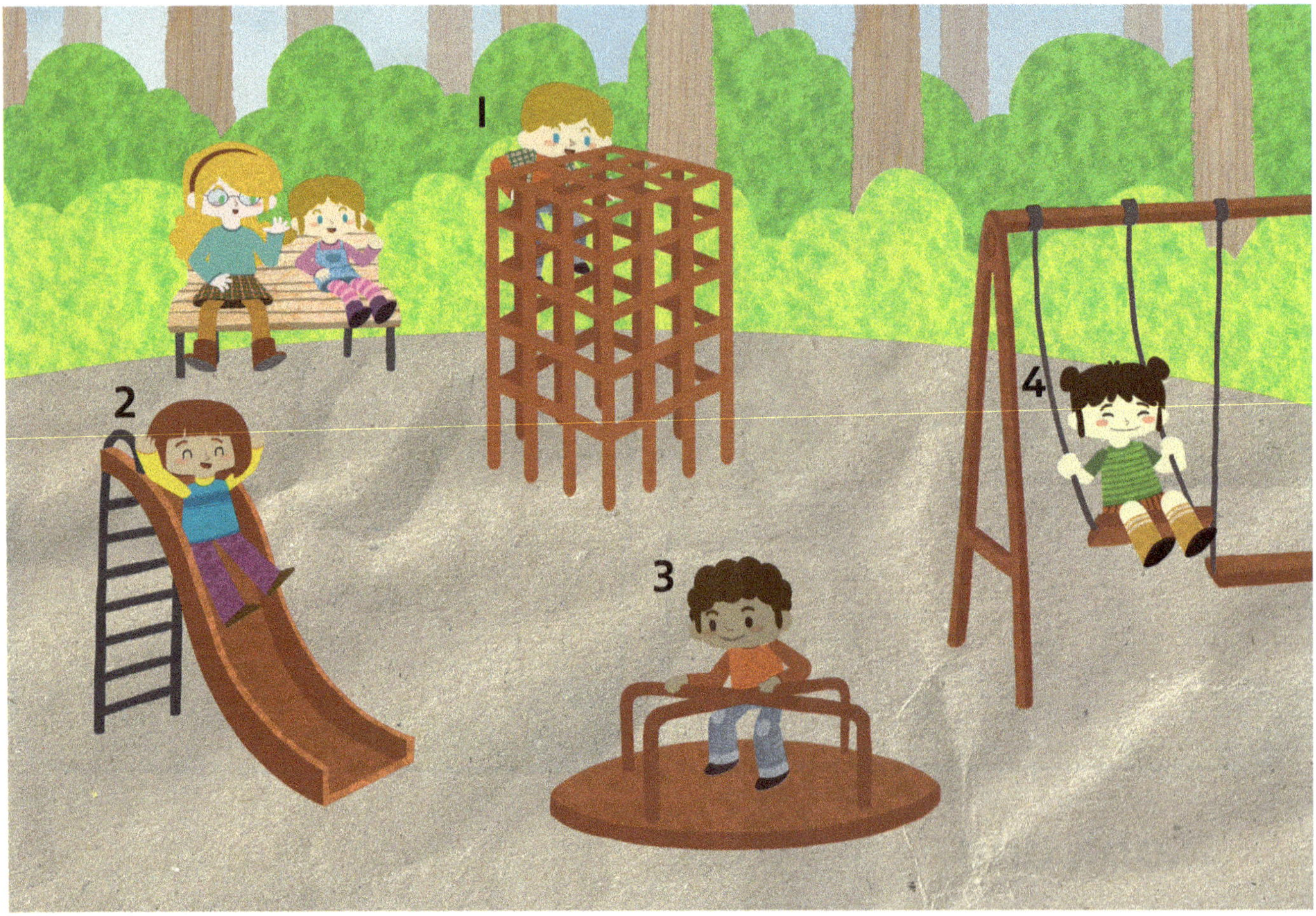

9 Listen and circle.

1 a b

2 a b

3 a b

4 a b

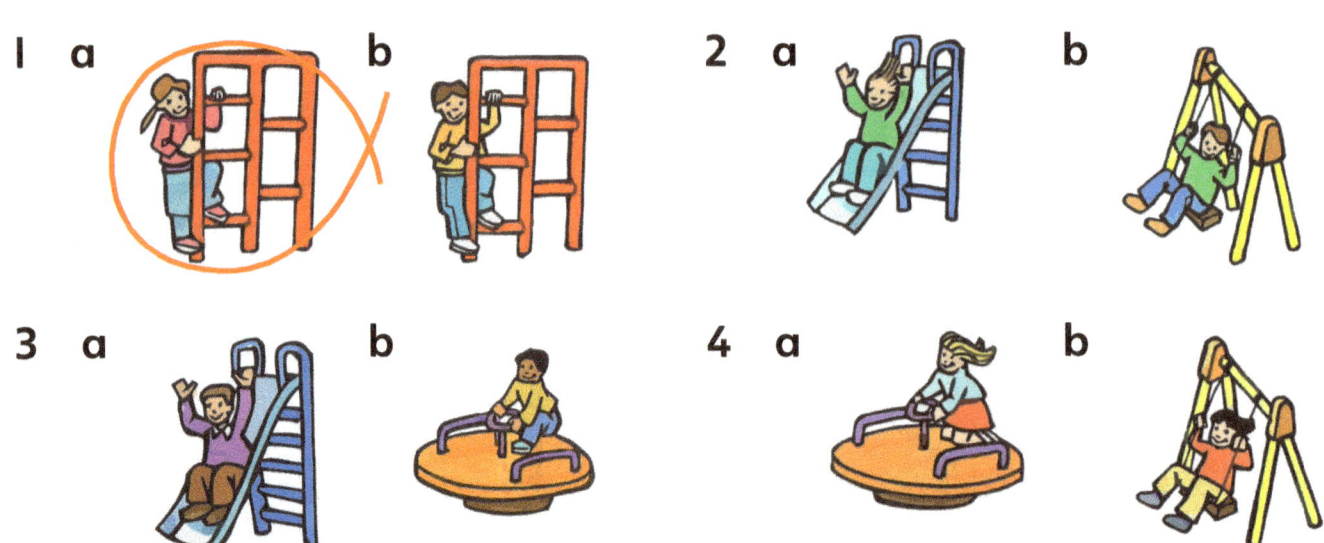

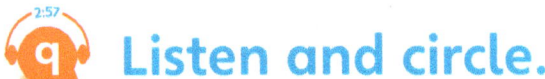

10 Listen and number. Say.

a

b

c

d

11 Mime and guess.

Review

12 **Look and number.**

13 **Play. Ask and answer. Then number.**

 Listen and number.

1

2

3  **1**

4

Listen and ✓ or ✗.

1  ✓

2

3

4

 **I Can**

unit 7 It's sunny!

3:01
1 Listen, look and say.

3:02
2 Listen and find.   **3** Play a game.

4 Listen and find. Sing. 🎵

5 Listen and number. Say.

a

b

c  1

d

THINK BIG   Find the odd one out.

Story

6 Listen and follow. What's the weather like?

1

2

3

4

5

6

7 Listen and number.

a

b

c

story Unit 7 59

Language in Action

8 Listen. Help Liam and Lidya.

9 Listen and circle.

1 a 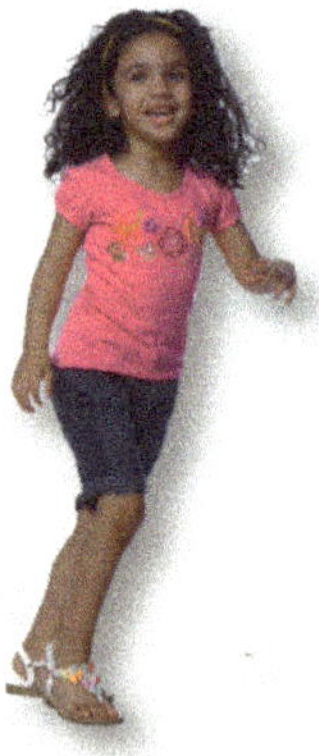

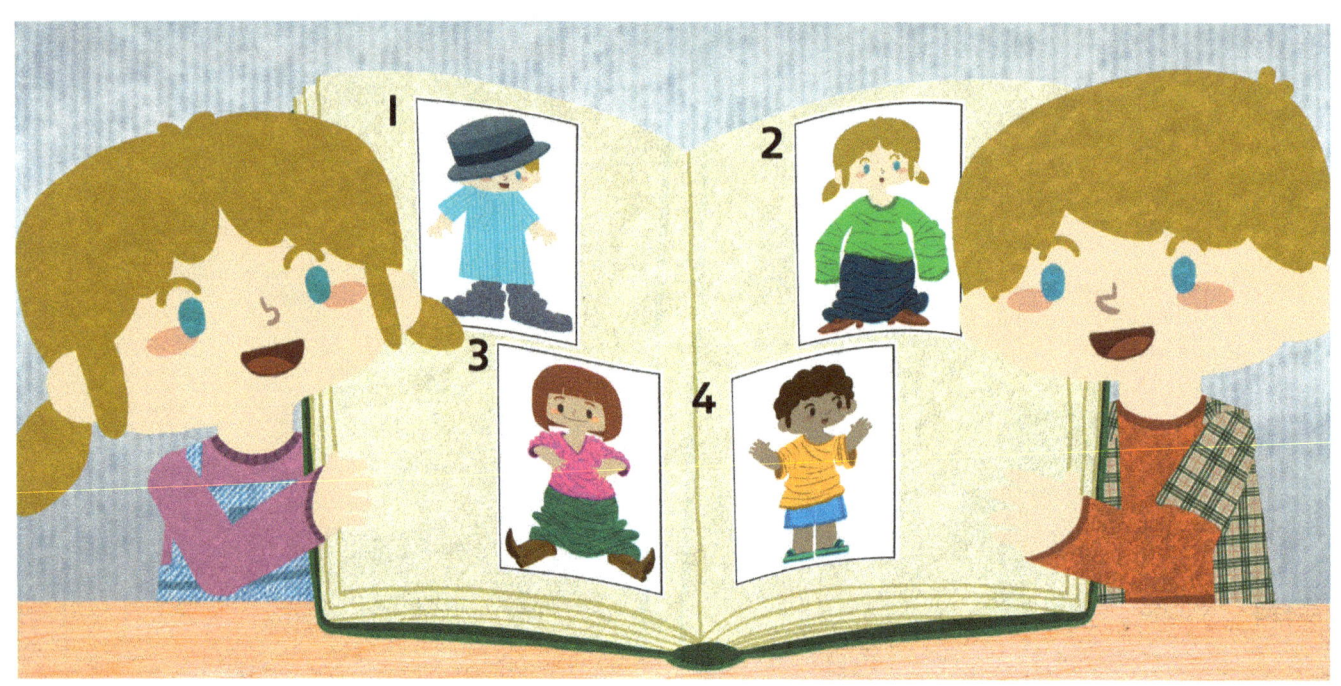

b 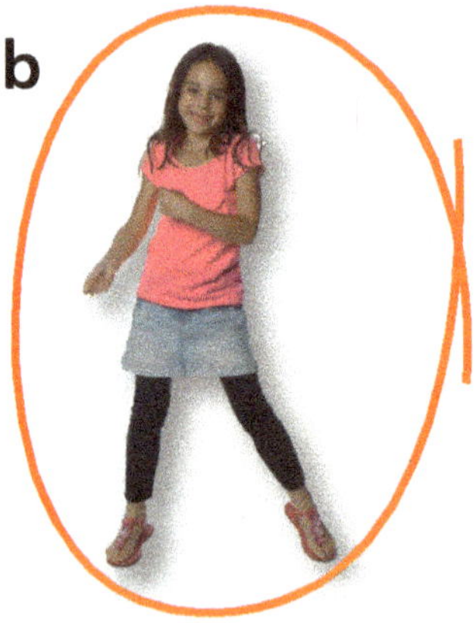

2 a 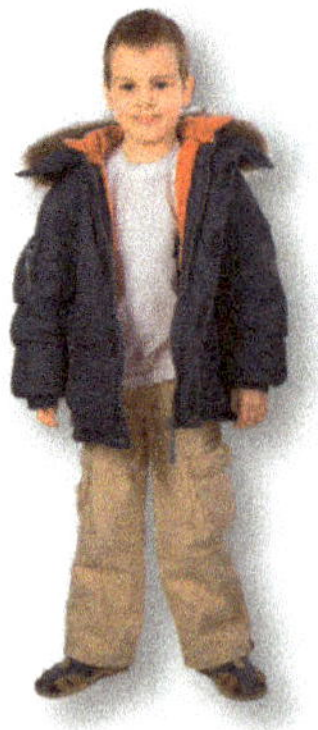

b 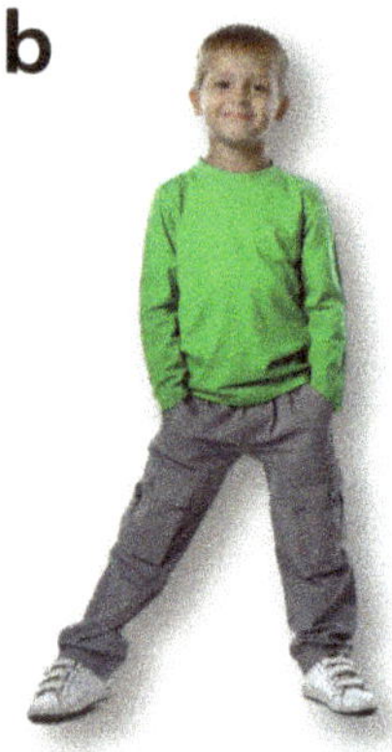

3 a 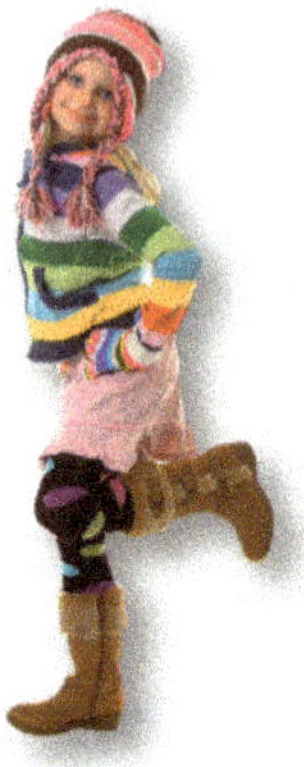

b 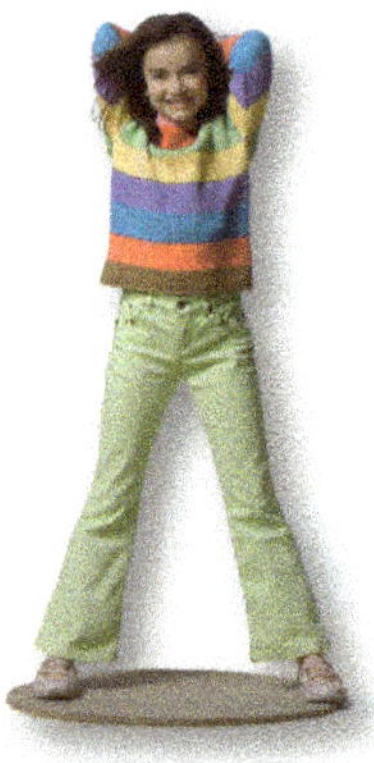

4 a 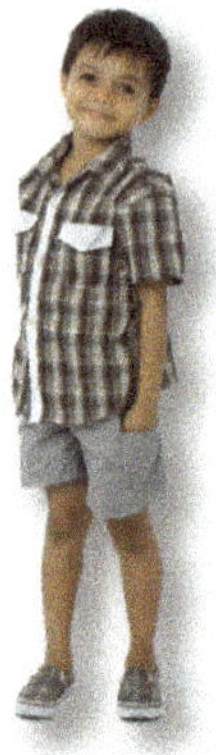

b 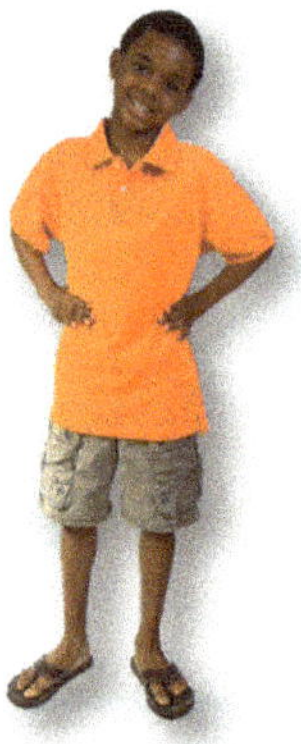

10 🎧 Listen and ✓. Play.

1

2

3

4

11 💬 Draw and say.

Review

12 Listen and follow. Say the colour.

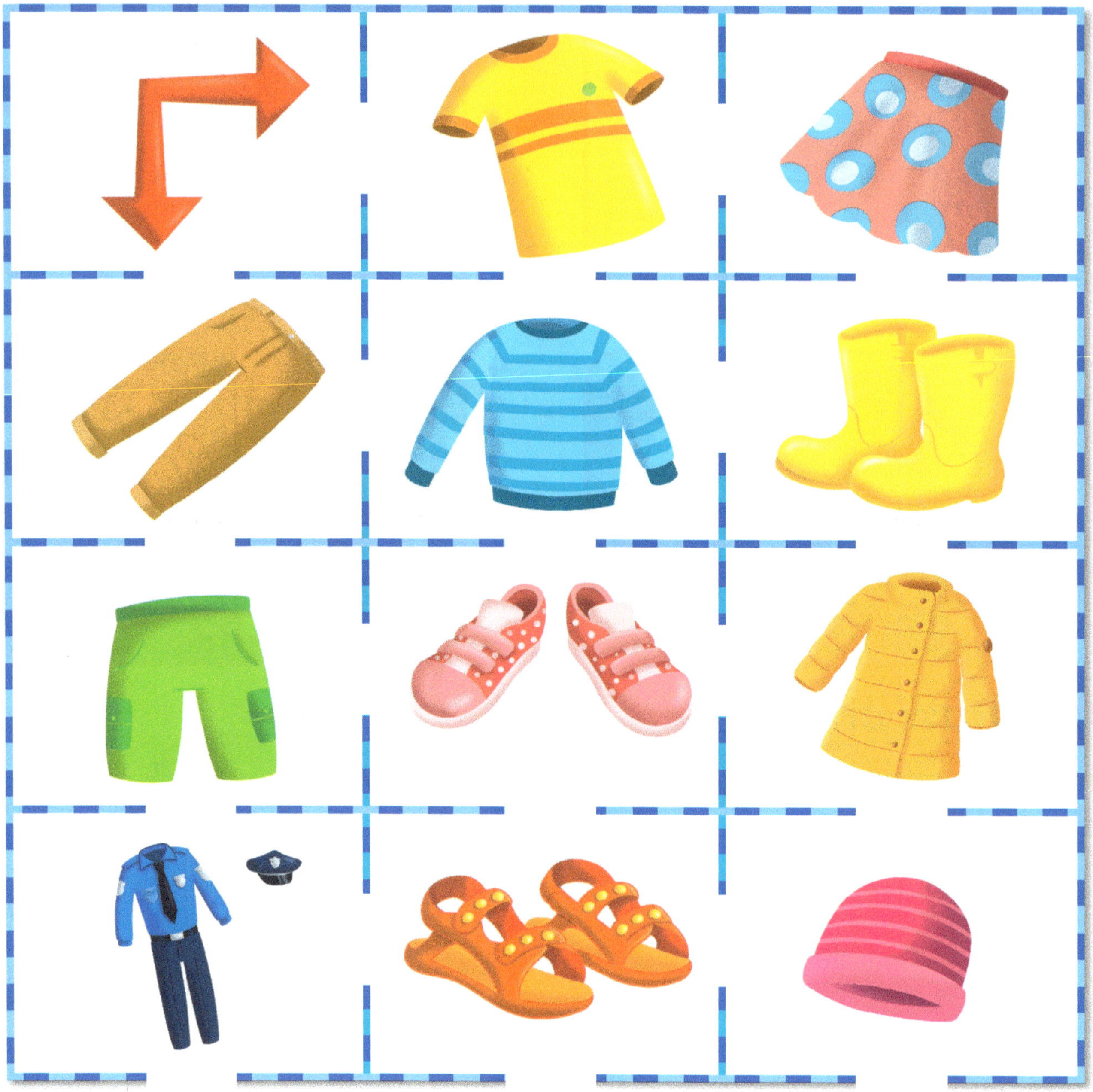

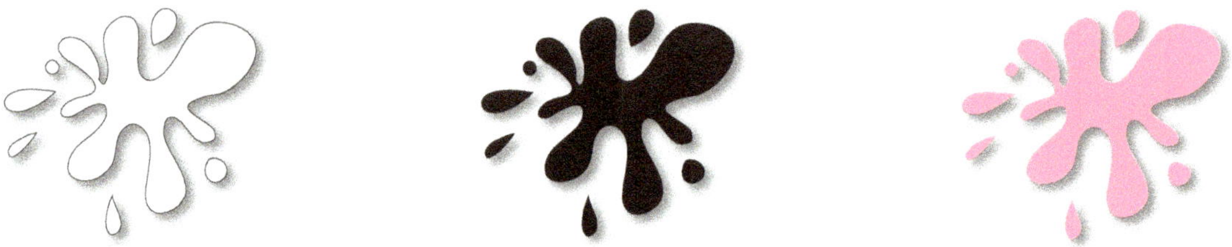

13 Play.

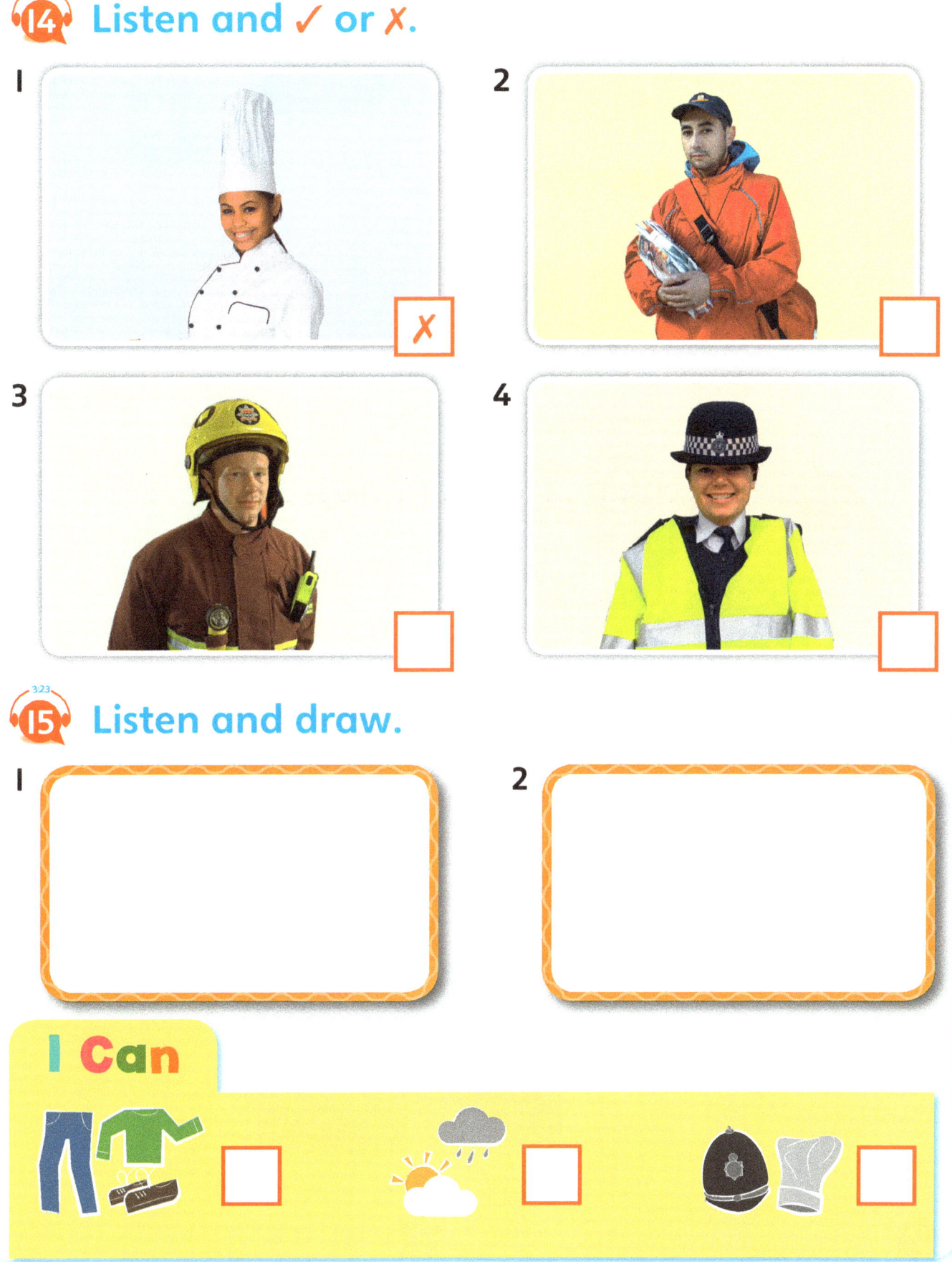

14 Listen and ✓ or ✗.

1   ✗

2

3

4

15 Listen and draw.

1

2

I Can

1 Listen, look and say.

2 Listen and find. 3 Play a game.

 **4** **Listen and sing. Number in order.**

 5 **Listen and circle. Say the room.**

1 a   b
2 a   b
3 a   b
4 a   b

THINK BIG   **Find the odd one out.**

Story

6 Listen and follow. Where's Lidya?

 7 **Listen and ✓ or ✗.**

1
 ✓

2

3

4

Language in Action

 8 **Listen. Help Lidya and Liam.**

 **9** **Listen and match.**

1 　2 　3 　4

a 　b 　c 　d

10 Draw Liam, Joy and you.
Ask and answer.

11 Ask and answer. Where are you?

Me			
1			
2			
3			

Listen and find.

1	2	3
4	5	6
7	8	q

13 **Play. Draw x or o.**

Listen and number.

a  ☐

b  ☐

c  **I**

d  ☐

Listen and draw.

 I Can

 ☐    ☐    ☐

A fish can swim!

1 Listen, look and say.

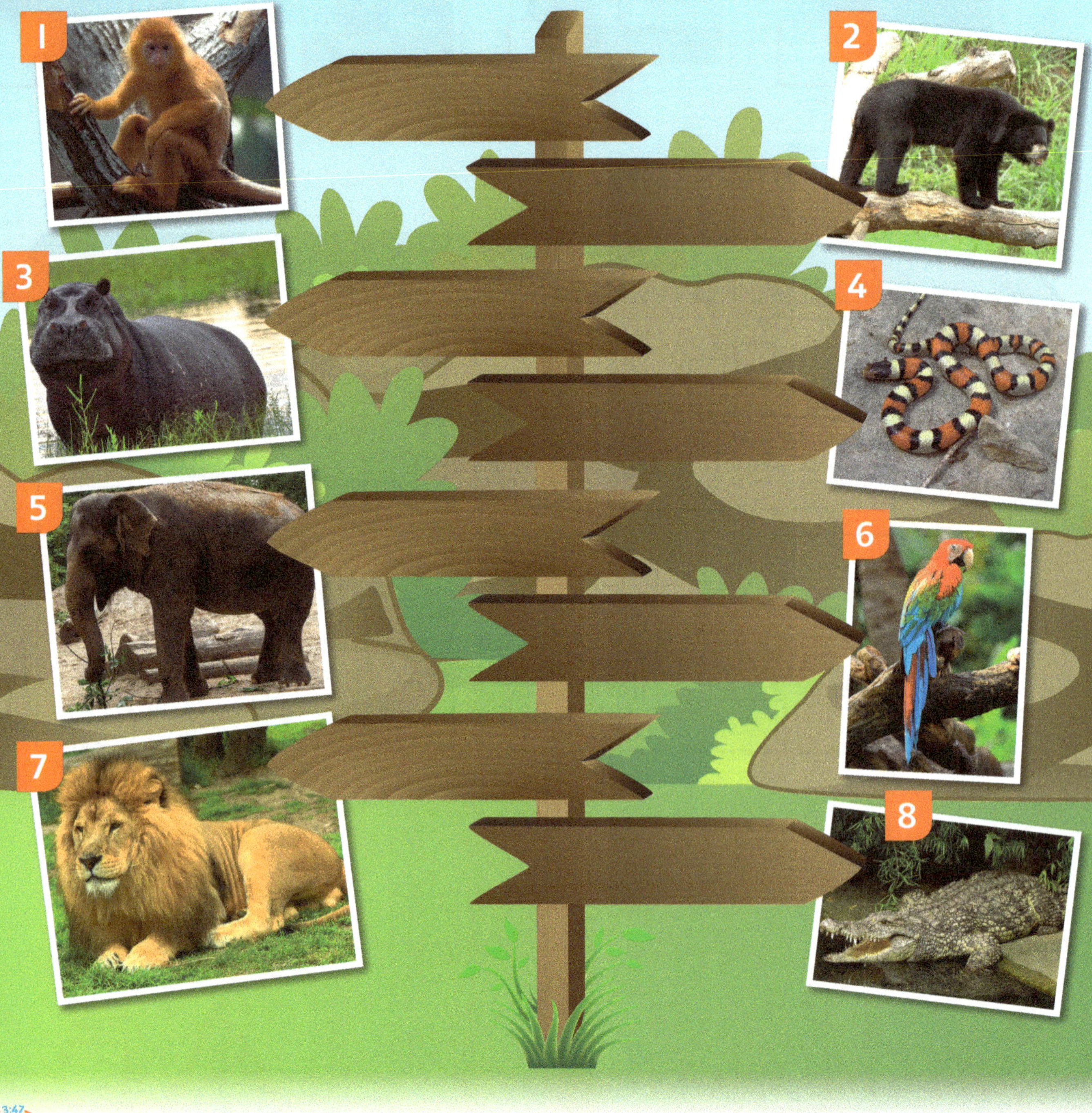

1

2

3

4

5

6

7

8

2 Listen and find.   **3** Play a game.

4 Listen and sing. What's missing? ♪

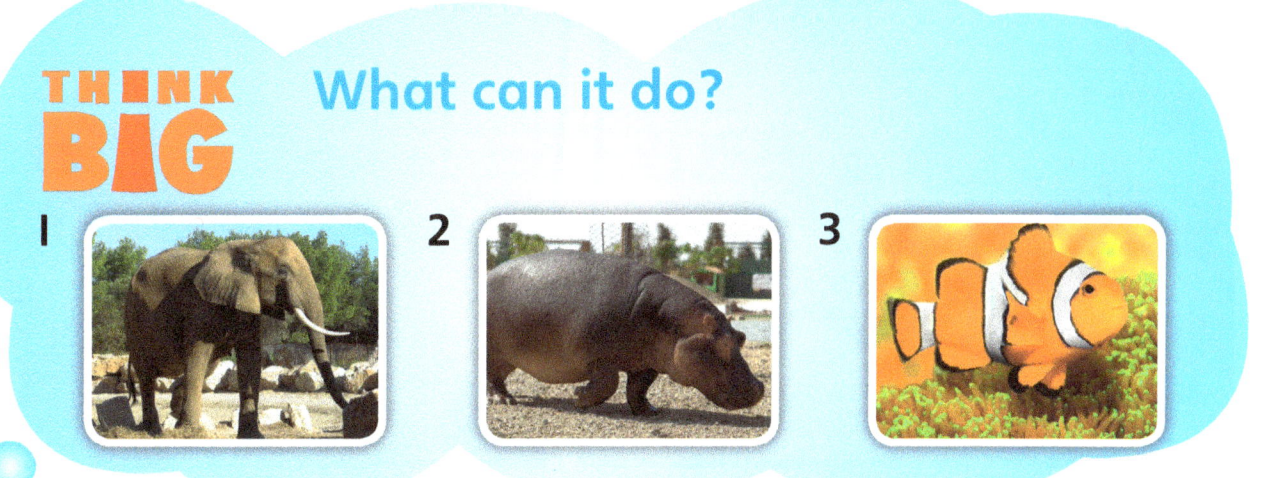

5 Listen and number. Say.

  1

THINK BIG   What can it do?

1 2 3

Story

6 Listen and follow. Where's Lidya?

7 Look and ✓ or ✗. Say.

1

✓

2

3

4

8 **Listen. Help Lidya and Liam.**

9 **Circle ✓ or ✗. Listen and check.**

Language in Action

10 Listen and play.

3:56

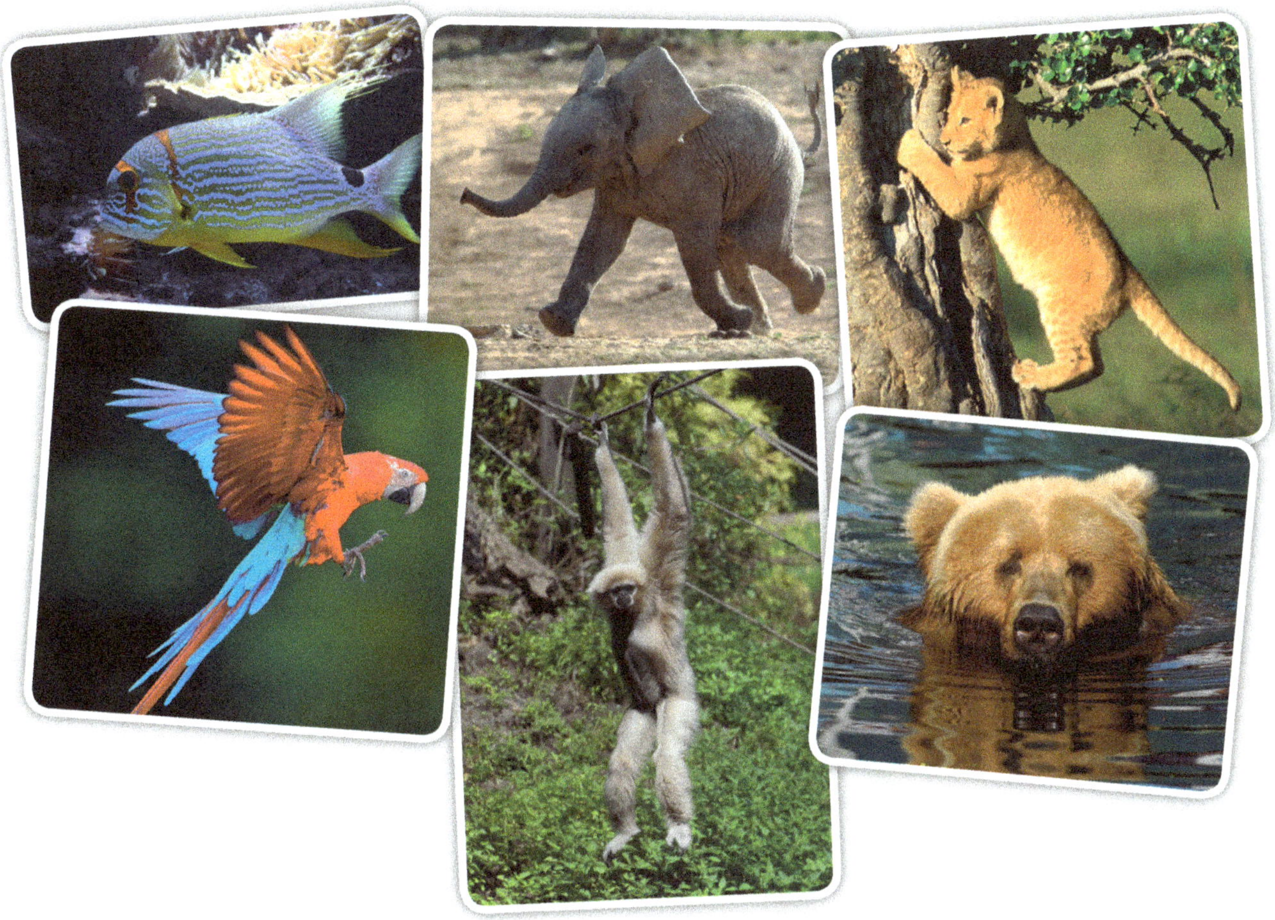

11 Draw and say.

12 Listen and ✓ or ✗. Play.

3:64 **Listen and match.**

1

2

3

4

a

b

c

d

 3:65 **Listen and number.**

a

b

c

d

[ ]

[ ]

[1]

[ ]

I Can

[ ] [ ] [ ]

Pearson Education Limited

Edinburgh Gate

Harlow

Essex CM20 2JE

England

and Associated Companies throughout the world.

www.pearsonelt.com/bigenglish

First published 2014

ISBN: 978-1-4479-9487-9

Set in Lab Avenir

Acknowledgements

The publisher would like to thank the following for their kind permission to reproduce their photographs:

(Key: b-bottom; c-centre; l-left; r-right; t-top)

Alamy Images: John Angerson 63tr, Bailey-Cooper Photography 53 (c), By Ian Miles-Flashpoint Pictures 47/3, Chris Cooper-Smith 63br, DWD-photo 47/6, DWImages Europe 47/4, Ingram Publishing 72/1, 76, Ingram Publishing 72/1, 76, Peter Jordan_NE 40/6, Justin Kase zsixz 47/2, macana 40/5, Borislav Marinic 48tr, MBI 13, Mark Richardson 47/1, Maria Wachala 40/7, Kevin Wheal 40/1; **Corbis:** Blend Images / Jose Luis Pelaez, Inc. 9/4 (top left), 15/1, Blend Images / Jose Luis Pelaez, Inc. 9/4 (top left), 15/1, Laura Doss 1c, Laura Doss 1c, Randy Faris 1cl, Randy Faris 1cl, Flint 53 (d), Jose Luis Pelaez, Inc 21/2, 23 (f), Jose Luis Pelaez, Inc 21/2, 23 (f), Neumann & Rodtmann 12/4, Ocean 8cl, 53 (b), 55/3, 56br, Ocean 8cl, 53 (b), 55/3, 56br, Ocean 8cl, 53 (b), 55/3, 56br, Ocean 8cl, 53 (b), 55/3, 56br, Tetra Images / Sarah M. Golonka 12/3, 15/5, Tetra Images / Sarah M. Golonka 12/3, 15/5, Wavebreak Media LTD 1cr, Wavebreak Media LTD 1cr; **DK Images:** Carolyn Barber 64/3, 68 (c), Carolyn Barber 64/3, 68 (c), Dave King 16/4, 16/5, Dave King 16/4, 16/5, Stephen Oliver 16/6, 23 (a), Stephen Oliver 16/6, 23 (a); **Fotolia.com:** A.Drean 73 (parrot), 77bl, A.Drean 73 (parrot), 77bl, Africa Studio 24/3, 24/7, Africa Studio 24/3, 24/7, alisonhancock 71 (c), amelie 77bc, anankkml 72/2, apops 63tl, ask4more 72 (crocodile), 72/8, 79/4, ask4more 72 (crocodile), 72/8, 79/4, ask4more 72 (crocodile), 72/8, 79/4, AVAVA 68/1, bakerjim 28/4, bst2012 68/2, 68/4, bst2012 68/2, 68/4, Cyril Comtat 72/7, 79/3, Cyril Comtat 72/7, 79/3, dark_didier 73/1, ep stock 40/2, erasdesign 24/4, 31/4, erasdesign 24/4, 31/4, Petro Feketa 48tl, 55/4, Petro Feketa 48tl, 55/4, Eric Gevaert 77br, ingridd313 72/3, 79/1, ingridd313 72/3, 79/1, iofoto 71 (b), kamonrat 72/6, karandaev 31/3, Kletr 73/3, Vera Kuttelvaserova 31/1, Kzenon 48 (a), 53/1, Kzenon 48 (a), 53/1, legaa 28/1, Liaurinko 24/8, 31/6, Liaurinko 24/8, 31/6, lunamarina 73 (lion), Paul Maguire 64/5, 64/7, 65r, 68 (a), Paul Maguire 64/5, 64/7, 65r, 68 (a), Paul Maguire 64/5, 64/7, 65r, 68 (a), Paul Maguire 64/5, 64/7, 65r, 68 (a), mattjeppson 72/4, 79/2, mattjeppson 72/4, 79/2, Marco Mayer 28/3, 31/2, Marco Mayer 28/3, 31/2, Mny-Jhee 28/2, Monkey Business 8tr, 21/1, 23 (b), Monkey Business 8tr, 21/1, 23 (b), Monkey Business 8tr, 21/1, 23 (b), Duncan Noakes 77tc, nvelichko 73 (monkey), Oez 16/1, 23 (c), Oez 16/1, 23 (c), okinawakasawa 24/6, Pixmax 77tl, Rob 68/3, Fabio Roncaglia 73/2, SergiyN 7/4, Sharpshot 71 (d), Iriana Shiyan 64/2, 64/6, 65l, 68 (b), 68 (d), Iriana Shiyan 64/2, 64/6, 65l, 68 (b), 68 (d), Iriana Shiyan 64/2, 64/6, 65l, 68 (b), 68 (d), Iriana Shiyan 64/2, 64/6, 65l, 68 (b), 68 (d), Iriana Shiyan 64/2, 64/6, 65l, 68 (b), 68 (d), Comugnero Silvana 24/2, sixore 72/5, Nikolai Sorokin 16/2, 23 (e), Nikolai Sorokin 16/2, 23 (e), Soyka 60/2 (b), stootsy 24/5, trekandshoot 64/4, Viktor 24/1, 31/5, Viktor 24/1, 31/5, Eugen Wais 16/3, wazymodo 48bl, 55/2, wazymodo 48bl, 55/2; **Getty Images:** Britain On View / Eric Nathan 63bl, Muriel de Seze 71 (a), Fotosearch 12/2, 15/4, Fotosearch 12/2, 15/4, Fuse 9/4 (centre right), 9/5 (1), Fuse 9/4 (centre right), 9/5 (1), Fuse 9/4 (centre right), 9/5 (1), Fuse 9/4 (centre right), 9/5 (1), Glow Images, Inc 9/4 (top right), 9/5 (3), Glow Images, Inc 9/4 (top right), 9/5 (3), Glow Images, Inc 9/4 (top right), 9/5 (3), Glow Images, Inc 9/4 (top right), 9/5 (3), Leigh Howell Love 8cr, huronphoto 60/3 (a), joSon 15/6, Jupiterimages 9/4 (centre left), 9/5 (4), 15/2, Jupiterimages 9/4 (centre left), 9/5 (4), 15/2, Jupiterimages 9/4 (centre left), 9/5 (4), 15/2, Jupiterimages 9/4 (centre left), 9/5 (4), 15/2, Jupiterimages 9/4 (centre left), 9/5 (4), 15/2, Rob Lewine 60/3 (b), Photodisc 12 (girl), Doug Schneider 32, 60/4 (b), Doug Schneider 32, 60/4 (b), Stockbyte 21/3, 23 (d), Stockbyte 21/3, 23 (d), Elke Van de Velde 9/4 (bottom right), View Pictures / UIG via **Getty Images** 40/4; **Imagestate Media:** Paul Goldstein 77tr; **MedioImages:** 9/4 (bottom left), 9/5 (2), 9/4 (bottom left), 9/5 (2); **Pearson Education Ltd:** Trevor Clifford 8b, 9/4 (bottom centre), Trevor Clifford 8b, 9/4 (bottom centre), Terry Leung, Pearson Education Asia Ltd 16/7; **Pearson Education Ltd:** Trevor Clifford 7/1, 7/2, 7/3, 7/5, 7/6, Trevor Clifford 7/1, 7/2, 7/3, 7/5, 7/6, Trevor Clifford 7/1, 7/2, 7/3, 7/5, 7/6, Trevor Clifford 7/1, 7/2, 7/3, 7/5, 7/6, Trevor Clifford 7/1, 7/2, 7/3, 7/5, 7/6; **PhotoDisc:** Kevin Peterson 36 (a), 78/2, Kevin Peterson 36 (a), 78/2; **Rex Features:** Michael McGurk 40/3; **Shutterstock.com:** Nate Allred 56tl, Donald Joski 36 (d), 78/1, Donald Joski 36 (d), 78/1, E. Petersen 64/8, 65c, E. Petersen 64/8, 65c, Hurst Photo 47/5, Dan Kosmayer 60/4 (a), kurhan 12/1, Osokina Liudmila 56tr, Monkey Business Images 8tl, 15/3, 21/4, Monkey Business Images 8tl, 15/3, 21/4, Monkey Business Images 8tl, 15/3, 21/4, ostill 36 (c), 78/4, ostill 36 (c), 78/4, Pavel L Photo and Video 60/2 (a), vvvita 36 (b), 78/3, vvvita 36 (b), 78/3; **SuperStock:** Blend Images 60/1 (b), Citizen Stock 60/1 (a), Fancy Collection 1l, Fancy Collection 1l, RubberBall 1r, RubberBall 1r, UpperCut Images 56bl

Cover images: Front: Corbis: Laura Doss c, Laura Doss c, Randy Faris cl, Randy Faris cl, Wavebreak Media LTD cr, Wavebreak Media LTD cr; **SuperStock:** Fancy Collection l, Fancy Collection l, RubberBall r, RubberBall r

All other images © Pearson Education

Every effort has been made to trace the copyright holders and we apologise in advance for any unintentional omissions. We would be pleased to insert the appropriate acknowledgement in any subsequent edition of this publication.